Life Without God

A Guide To Fulfillment Without Religion

Nicolaos S. Tzannes, Ph.D

PublishAmerica
Baltimore

First printing

ISBN: 1-59129-769-9
PUBLISHED BY AMERICA HOUSE BOOK PUBLISHERS
www.publishamerica.com
Baltimore

Printed in the United States of America

Dedication

To all our genes, our masters
this book I dedicate.

They cause
the great dilemmas,
I'm destined to debate.

Dangling there from end to end,
within the genome strand,
they rule our moves, our senses,
and all we understand

N. S. Tzannes

Acknowledgment

I want to express my sincere thanks to my wife Estelita Marie. She not only served as my debating opponent during most of the conversations of this work, but she also read and edited the manuscript several times, coming up with many valuable suggestions in the process. And all that is in addition to tolerating me for more than forty years of marriage.

Table of Contents

PROLOGUE

I have never been able to accept the notion of a supreme being. Myriads of proselytizing efforts by my religious friends have failed to convert me. To this day I consider involvement in an organized religion a waste of my precious time.

In writing this guide, I have two objectives in mind.

The first one is to demonstrate the absurdity of religious dogmas, beliefs and practices. Every good non-believer, freethinker, atheist, agnostic, rationalist or non-theist needs the arguments developed in this part—they are the necessary ammunition for facing down religious zealots and annoying proselytizers. I am not claiming that all these arguments are original [9,10,23][1], but I think most of them are.

The second is to propose a simple but meaningful set of beliefs for those who sense that they have a mission in life, but are unable to accept the existence of a supreme being. In this part I put forth answers to questions such as "why are we here?" "how should we live our lives?" "what is good or evil?" "how do we find happiness?" etc., questions that have tormented humans since they began reflecting on their own existence. I believe that the articulated creed—which I have named Neo-humanism—demonstrates that opportunistic messiahs, self-serving cult leaders and other assorted exploiters of the human longing for faith are totally redundant. And that happiness and fulfillment in life are attainable without religion.

To avoid pedantry, the ideas are introduced simply and without the usual philosophical jargon. All topics are developed via conversations—the Socratian Dialogue approach. These conversations are quite sharp and heated, but not totally void of humor. Though proper referencing is maintained throughout the

---

[1] Numbers in parenthesis refer to the section *References and Notes* at the end of the book.

book, scholarship is not the primary motive here. Unlike most books on such subjects, it is written for the layman—one does not need a Ph.D to understand it. And that is what sets it apart from existing heavy treatises on the meaning of life. You will get simple, straight answers here—not references to famous philosophers, or skillful verbal acrobatics.

I am firmly convinced that the proposed ideas have a natural truth in them—that I am not proposing something new, but I am just revealing what's always there. This natural truth did not come to me by some spiritual epiphany—a book on how to live without god conceived by divine intervention would be the ultimate oxymoron. The truth is there for anyone to see—anyone who is not blinded by religion, of course.

Nicolaos S. Tzannes
June 2002

1

THE CASE
AGAINST THE DIVINE

It was more than 45 years ago when I decided to stop believing in a supreme being. I wasn't an apostate, mind you—my brain refused to accept the concept. All I'd been doing was pretending—just to fit in with my contemporaries. So, when I finally decided to take the plunge, it wasn't a big step—just the final formality. I simply pronounced openly what I harbored within me—that from now on I was a declared non-believer.

Time went by, and I suffered no ill effects from this pronouncement. I often affirmed my complete rejection of god in the *presence of witnesses*—my friends—just to see if any calamities would be thrown my way. Nothing! As my conversations with believers became more and more agitated, I would *blaspheme* using some rather unmentionable epithets for god—just to dare him to act, if he were really there. Still nothing! Not only that. My life remained a happy, satisfying and joyous one until today. Oh, sure, there were times of hardship—no life can be complete without its share of that. But I never considered them punishment from above for being an infidel, and I never asked for any help through prayer. In fact, my ability to cope with all my tribulations without ever converting to a believer solidified my conviction that he does not exist—that he is merely a figment of religious people's imagination.

By and by, I became quite comfortable with the notion that things were as I suspected. The logical arguments about the impossibility of god's existence that I read or *invented* myself became my new reality. *There is no god and it is somewhere else that I must turn to for meaning in my life*, I whispered often, while my mind worked unconsciously to formulate a new philosophy of existence.

In this first chapter I have recorded a number of conversations that I've had over the years with people of faith—Christians, for the most part. These conversations are heated debates of well-known religious dogmas, matters of religiosity and spirituality, and *proofs* of the existence of god. Their conclusions—with minor alterations—are also applicable to most other major religions whose central theme is the belief in an all-powerful being.[2] They have been embellished somewhat to make them more entertaining.

Since I am authoring them, I am usually the one who has the last word—the one who wins the arguments. However, winning or losing such intellectual skirmishes does not alter human behavior, as will become apparent in the sequel. It is, nevertheless, an ephemeral pleasure that does wonders for your self-esteem.

---

[2] Hinduism and Buddhism emphasize meditation rather than a belief in a single God (see references 40-44).

Who Voted For Them, Anyway?

"Democracy and religion are incompatible—they don't mix," I started, hoping to get immediate reaction from father Akakios, a priest in the Greek Orthodox Church in Minneapolis, Minnesota.

I was a student in Electrical Engineering at the University of Minnesota at the time—late nineteen fifties. The occasion was a wedding reception. Father Akakios had the misfortune of being seated next to me at the dinner table. It was early in my career as an armchair religious debater, so I was delighted to have the opportunity to test my skills. I had already prepared the topic for just such an eventuality, so I should have the logistical advantage.

Father Akakios, a theologian, was reputed to have also earned a Master's degree in political science. I figured he'd welcome a spirited exchange in his two fields.

"This could be an issue in the old country, Greece," he replied. "But here in the U.S. there is complete separation of church and state. You ought to know that, if you are a student at the university," he added with a patronizing smile.

"I do know of the separation of church and state in the United States—I took Political Science as a humanities elective," I replied. His slight smile meant that he was underestimating me, and that's how I wanted it. "But I was talking about the structure of organized religions. I think that as institutions, they are totally anachronistic and undemocratic. United States, which prides itself in being *the omphalos of democracy*, needs vibrant, democratic institutions for its continued vitality."

"Anachronistic and undemocratic? The Churches are full, in case you haven't noticed. The hunger for religion has never waned, even in the communist countries where it is outlawed. And you call them anachronistic?"

"The demand is there, I grant you," I replied. "But that hardly qualifies them as a modern democratic institution."

"What sort of democracy do you expect? Do you want a public referendum on the ten commandments?" He countered laughingly.

"That would be a good start," I replied. "And let me tell you something. The first one[3] will certainly be defeated as undemocratic. It is nothing but a stark declaration of a dictatorship, quite reminiscent of modern day military coups. God declares himself the only god as a personal reward for having saved the Jews from bondage. The next three may also suffer a similar fate. As for the one that demands that the Sabbath be holy, that's been done away with decades ago."

His face seemed to twist as if he was trying to recall the contents of the commandments. I sensed an advantage and pressed on with the assault.

"Then you have the parish priests or ministers—the local religious leaders. Who voted for them, anyway? They were appointed by some bishop or other who in turn was appointed by some archbishop, who was appointed by a pope or patriarch, none of whom were ever elected by anyone. Am I right or not?"

"You are wrong. The Patriarchs and Popes are usually elected by a Synod of Archbishops."

"Fine, but since those guys were never elected by the faithful, it is hardly what you call *representative* democracy. It is more like an oligarchy—another anachronistic institution if I am not mistaken."

Father Akakios started to fidget with a piece of lettuce left in his salad bowl. He appeared annoyed to have been squeezed to this uncomfortable, defensive position.

"And then there is the offensive verbiage—the religious titles," I continued mercilessly. "The Churches insist on calling their bishops *Excellencies*. They continue to refer to god as *The Lord*. What is that all about, if not undemocratic? Isn't it time they recognized that these titles of European aristocracy have no place in a democratic society? That they are the very things that our forefathers died to eliminate?"

"You may have a valid point about the lack of democracy in the Church. After all, the head of the Church is God—all powerful and

---

[3] "I am the Lord thy God, which have brought thee out of the land of Egypt, out of the house of bondage. Thou shalt have no other gods before me."

forever—with no term limits, or the possibility of impeachment," a recovered father Akakios remarked with a hint of amusement. "Do you really think we should open up *his post* to worldwide elections," he asked sarcastically.

"Well, he made that pretty near impossible by adding that commandment that forbids people to use his name in vain—whatever that means. How can you have a fair election without a candidate's ability to mention his opponent's name? That's the sort of mind set that has crept down the hierarchical structure of the church, causing a lot of damage to the population."

"What are you talking about? What sort of damage?

"All the democratic institutions (schools, the press, mass media, etc.) devote a lot of effort educating the citizenry—especially young minds—on democratic principles. Then the unsuspected faithful walk into their churches and it is like going from day to night. Dictatorship rules supreme, damaging or undoing with one stroke endless hours of civic education. I tell you, organized religions, the product of a bygone era, are stagnant, authoritarian—a blatant affront to democracy, to say the least."

"Your last parataxis is insulting," father Akakios interrupted sternly. "You are nearing the edge—about to cross over to the realm of blasphemy."

"Blasphemy! Oh, yeah—thanks for reminding me. That's how religions do away with an individual's freedom of speech, right?"

With that, Father Akakios called the hostess, and I was politely escorted out through the front door. That's the way it goes.

You go against the predominant way of thinking, and you quickly become a pariah.

Do You Believe In the Electron?

"I find it hard to believe in a supreme being that I've never seen," I asserted. "I have repeatedly challenged him to come out of hiding and show himself to me—even once—but to no avail. I have even *blasphemed*, daring him to punish me for it. No response, he appears to ignore me—I can't but conclude that he is completely fictitious. As for the people who claim that they have visions of the divine, I think they are either dishonest, or hallucinatory. And by the way, I am only referring to god as if he were a male, because that is the usual practice. As far as I am concerned he doesn't exist as either of the two prime genders, or any of the secondary ones—not even as an…it."

"What?" Norman P., a university colleague with deep Catholic convictions, responded, somewhat annoyed with my last remarks. "Are you saying that you believe only in things that you can see?"

"You wouldn't expect me to devote my entire life to a god whose existence is questionable," I replied. "I need some tangible proof. Seeing him would be such a proof."

"But I know for a fact that you believe that an electron exists, even though you've never seen one. If you deny it, you are not only a liar, but a hypocrite as well. You have been teaching electrical engineering for years now, and the electron is sprinkled throughout your lecture notes." He had the *I gotcha* look on his face.

"I don't deny that I believe that an electron exists, even though I have never seen one," I replied. "I also believe that the water out of the faucet comes from some reservoir that I have never seen; that the earth is round though I have never actually seen it. I could mention a number of other things, but I don't want to bore you."

"Then why don't you believe in God? Is there some innate prejudice or are you doing it for its shock effect?"

"Neither," I replied. "You see, the key word here is *believe*. When I say that I believe in the electron, I mean that I accept its existence, because it explains electrical phenomena. But I don't believe in the electron the same way *you want me to believe in god*. I don't *worship* the Electron! I don't *kneel and pray* to the Electron!

17

I don't *love or fear* the Electron! I don't *build temples* to the Electron! I don't pay part of my income to priests, bishops, and the like, who masquerade as earthly surrogates for the Electron. I do NOT live my life according to some Electron commandments. In short, I don't spend half of my waking hours thinking about the Electron's existence. If you want me to believe in your god the same way, I might oblige, but you wouldn't get any credit for converting me." Now I've got the *I gotcha* look on my face.

"Well, you are hopeless. At least I got you to admit that He may exist, even in this *electron sense* that you are describing. Let me tell you, though. Faith is a beautiful thing, and I am glad I have it. Every day I *thank God for granting me the honor of making me a believer.*"

"If you are right and he exists and he is responsible for our personality traits, should I also be thanking him for making me a non-believer?" I asked Norman, smiling. "I am not wasting my life worshiping him, and I don't have to thank him for anything. In fact, I am enjoying every minute of my life without his oppressive presence—happy as a lark, I might add. Don't you ever wonder why he allowed me to be free of the bondage he has placed on you? If you weren't blinded by faith, you'd realize that he has actually short-changed you."

Norman left that evening looking perplexed. He must have spent the night developing some new ideas, because he was knocking at my office door early the next morning.

Religion Is A Science

"You are not a real scientist unless you belong to an organized religion," he started without even saying *good morning*. "Religion is the perfect paradigm of a science and I am going to prove it to you today."

"Religion, a science?" I replied. "Isn't that an oxymoron?"

"We will see how you feel about that by the end of the debate," Norman replied. "For now, I challenge you to follow my train of thought and play the devil's advocate to the best of your ability. That shouldn't be hard, considering," he sneered sarcastically without completing the statement

"OK," I smiled, tacitly acknowledging his word pun, "but it'll have to wait until this evening. I have two consecutive classes this morning, and my afternoon is filled with office hours and committee meetings. Why don't you come over for dinner, and we can discuss it after the dessert."

"Fine," he replied. "I will bring the wine. I won't drink any of that cheap beer you always serve—it clouds the mind and weakens the debating skills."

"Make it a red, then. My wife, Estelle, is making beef burgundy for supper."

Later that evening, Norman showed up at the house holding up a good red Napa Valley wine. It wasn't long before supper was finished and we retired to the porch for dessert and coffee.

"OK," he began while unbuckling his belt, to better accommodate my Estelle's torte creation. "I want you to try to recall the rudiments of that course we both attended at the Johns Hopkins University—the one on *The Philosophy of Science* [36,37].[4] Do you remember it?"

"I recall taking the course," I replied. "But not that the course's contention was that religion is a science."

---

[4] The reader is reminded that numbers in parenthesis refer to the numbered references at the end of the book.

"Go easy on the sarcasm," Norman retorted. "I never said that the course did that. But I am going to use the course's methodology to do it myself."

"Is that so?"

"I remember well that a celebrated example of a scientific theory presented in the course was Plane Geometry—often called Euclidian Geometry after its originator, the Greek mathematician, Euclid. I'm sure that you remember that, considering that Euclid was one of your countrymen."

"I do recall Euclid and his Geometry. Did Euclid make the claim that religion is a science?"

"I am going to totally ignore your wisecracks, so that I can better concentrate on my development," Norman countered. "Now tell me, what comes first in the development of Euclidian Geometry? Is it not the definitions of some of the terms like a *point*, a *line*, etc?"

"Yes, it is," I replied. "To develop a scientific theory, you have to clearly define your terms. This is one of the problems with wannabe sciences like sociology, psychology, etc.—they cannot define precisely some of the basic terms like human intelligence and...."

"Sorry for interrupting, but we are not here to theorize on the shortfalls of these fields—save it for another day. Concentrate on my argument and tell me what comes next after the definitions. It is very important, perhaps the most important part of the development of a scientific theory. What is it?"

"Hmm, was it the postulates or axioms?"

"You bet," he said excitedly. "So a scientific theory is a collection of terms and their definitions, a set of axioms, and then statements in the form of theorems, corollaries and lemmas which derive from these axioms. The axioms represent the *mother* of the theory—the source of all that follows. Am I right, or not?"

"Yes," I replied. "So how is your religion—Catholicism—a *scientific theory*? Where are your terms and their definitions? Where are your axioms?"

"Easy," Norman replied, his face flushed with exhilaration. "The terms are God, the Vatican, the Pope, the Bishops, etc. The definitions of the terms spell out their positions, their powers, their duties and the hierarchical structure of the Church, i.e. the interrelationships among themselves and the people. There are very precise definitions of these things in the Catholic Church, you know. Anything wrong so far?"

"Intriguing," I said. Where are your axioms?"

"The first axiom is that God is all powerful, and that he created the cosmos, continuing to exercise control over it. The second is that the Pope, the head of the church, is infallible—God inspires all that he asserts, and it must be obeyed. The third is…"

"You don't have to go on," I interrupted. "The rest of your argument is obvious. You will next make the claim that all else—the rest of the church dogma—derives from these axioms, and bingo, we have the proof that Catholicism—a religion—is also a science."

"You better believe it, buster," he replied. He got up and approached me, raising his hands to receive some high fives. His excitement was so intense, it was surprising that he didn't start jumping up and down, sounding out the usual howls of victory.

"Well?" he asked me pointedly. "Are you ready to join? You will have to study a lot of stuff and pass some serious tests. We don't accept every walk-in, you know!"

"Not quite," I replied. "But so far, I got to say that you were good—very good. You got the terms and their definitions, a bunch of axioms and a seeming collection of *truths* derived sequentially from these axioms. Bingo—the scientific religion of Catholicism. Not bad! But will it stand the next stage of inquiry? The critical scrutiny?"

"I'm ready," replied Norman, taking on an expression of a boxer ready to counterpunch against a barrage of anticipated left/right combinations.

"For starters, I seem to recall that the axioms must be self-evident. The Euclidean axiom that only one parallel line can be drawn from a point to a line is self-evident. I won't challenge the existence of god—it appears to be self-evident to a lot of people—but what of the infallibility of the Pope?"

"Wait a minute," he protested. "The self-evident nature of the axioms has been done away with in modern scientific thought. The axioms are now viewed as a collection of statements, which form the foundation of the scientific theory—and that's all. Non-Euclidian Geometry, Einstein's theory of relativity, etc. have axioms that are far from self-evident—and you know it."

"You are right—I just wanted to see whether you are on the ball," I replied feebly, trying to cover up quickly for my blunder. "What about all the rules and regulations on living a Catholic life? How are they derived from the axioms? From what axiom do you derive the belief that you have to confess your sins to cleanse your soul? That you can't have an abortion? That you can't divorce your wife? That all priests must be male and remain celibate? And all the other arbitrary pronouncements of the Catholic Church?"

"Easy," he replied. "The Pope puts out an edict, and from the second axiom—the Pope is infallible—the edict is correct and it must be obeyed. Any other objections?"

"Hmm, clever—very clever," I replied thoughtfully.

"Is that all you are going to say?" he replied aghast. "Are you agreeing with me then?"

"Well, I am formulating my rebuttal," I replied after a brief silence. "I think that your axiom of infallibility, though a clever ruse, renders the theory… degenerate."

"What do you mean *degenerate*?" Norman shouted with fire in his eyes.

"Degenerate in a strictly mathematical sense," I replied quickly. "You know the definition of a degenerate case—obvious, trivial, of no scientific interest."

"Do you care to elaborate? How is the infallibility of the Holy See degenerate?" Norman shrieked.

"Yes, I do. Anyone—even a crackpot—can proclaim an axiom like *"I am all powerful and infallible, and anything I state is the truth,"* and then start spewing out any nonsense that passes through his mind. Theoretically, his pronouncements comprise a *single-axiom scientific theory*. He does not even have to build up the theory via lemmas, theorems, and the like—every statement is directly referenced to the foundational axiom—*he is always right*. Sort of like you just did, I mean—using your pope. But who cares? Who is going to take him seriously? The crackpot and his pronouncements are a *degenerate* theory—of no interest to the scientific community."

"Millions of people obey the Pope, and your implication that he might be a crackpot is vile," Norman protested.

"I never said he was a crackpot. I was elaborating on the nature of a degenerate scientific theory. In any event, I've got to congratulate you on your skillful manipulation of the methodology of the course. Considering that by definition religion is not a science, you came pretty close to proving the impossible."

Norman's eyes became glassy—he started to look dazed, exhausted.

"There is one more thing I want to say," I added a few minutes later, "and it pertains to the concept of the infallibility of your pope. How can anyone as smart as you subscribe to this preposterous notion that a human being can be infallible?"

"Because it leads to a...*perfect science*, that's why," Norman replied stubbornly.

Norman and I never talked about religion again. He gave up trying to convince me of the eternal truths of his faith, and I stopped trying to demonstrate the lack of logic in his convictions.

Persisting on either effort would have been futile.

On Life After Life

"You call religion a waste of time, yet you spent endless hours discussing it with your friends," my wife, Estelle, remarked one evening as we sat down for the after dinner coffee ritual. "That's *intellectual masturbation*—to use one of your own pet phrases. Who cares whether religion makes logical sense or not? The reason why people need religion in their life is…*death*!"

Estelle is a religious person and not particularly happy about this book project.

"Oh, really? They devote—*waste* is more to the point—their life to religion to cheat death?"

"Yes! Metaphorically speaking, of course!"

"I don't think I am getting the metaphor."

"Oh, come on, sure you are. They cheat death through religion because they *lose the fear of death*. You know very well that humans are the only creatures who are aware of their own mortality. This is a terrible burden and religion is there to ease it with its promise of an everlasting and blissful life, as a soul type entity. In short, religion reduces the fear of death and makes our life more bearable."

"I think this *fear of death* concept is highly overstated. Most young people I know think they are immortal and middle age people are too busy with families and career to think of death. The only people who even think of death are old people."

"My Jewish friends think of death all the time—that's all they talk about," Estelle hissed.

"OK, them too, then. The rest of the people only think of death when it is imminent."

"That's still everybody, then, just that they do it when death stares them in the face."

"And you think that when their time comes they are terrified and this fairy tale about heaven, angels, etc. eases their terror?"

"You've got a better suggestion on what happens after we die?"

"Not at this minute, but I'm working on it," I replied. "In the meantime I would opt for the truth."

"Which is?"

"That we don't know. Besides I don't agree that they are terrified. Most indications—from people who died but were revived—are that it was a happy state of mind, a light and comfortable eerie feeling. No terror."

"Religious people prefer the fairy tale—as you called it—rather than the uncertainty of what will happen after death."

"But the fairy tale is laughable—not to mention *stressful.*"

"Stressful?"

"One major religion[5] promises men who qualify that they will ascend to heaven as a spirit and 72 virgins will be waiting for them, primed for action. Isn't it stressful to know that you are offered 72 virgins but you have—being a spirit—no equipment to…de-virginize them?" I laughed.

"You like to ridicule every religious idea, don't you," Estelle complained.

I paused for a few seconds, and then I looked at Estelle straight in the eyes.

"Do you want to know what I really think of the promise of everlasting life in heaven? Of the suggestion that if you are free of sins, you are on your way to a perpetual bliss in some paradise?" I asked her sternly.

"Besides characterizing a fairy tale?"

"Yes! That it is reckless and irresponsible, possibly even bordering on criminality."

She stared at me with astonishment

"That you will have to explain. I have often heard you ramble on and on about crimes committed by religions in the name of God throughout history. But this new suggestion—this new accusation—that the promise of a better life after death is *criminal*, is a new low, even for you."

"I made it with a heavy heart," I replied. "And I was careful to attribute to it only the possibility of criminality. The reason that you have not heard it from me before is that I have only recently reached this conclusion."

"Really? Is there any particular reason why this new idea popped

---

[5] Islam

into your head?" she asked mockingly.

"Yes, recent events like the terrorist attack on the World Trade Center in New York, for example. I have just realized that terrorists murder innocents and kill themselves, all the while convinced that they are doing god's work, and believing firmly that they are headed for heaven. Whoever put such ideas into their head carries criminal responsibility, does he not?"

"He does, and that is why we consider the masterminds of the act also *terrorists*. But mainstream religions prohibit killing—in Christianity it is one of the commandments. So, where is their irresponsibility?"

"They are the originators of the idea of life after death. Look at it this way. Could you ever turn a non-believer into a terrorist? Very unlikely! There is no way you can convince him to perform any act that will get him to heaven—he does not believe in such a place. The logical conclusion is that suggestions of an afterlife are reckless and irresponsible, because they create religious terrorists. The notion that religions carry also criminal responsibility for terrorist acts is a bit farfetched, but a clever lawyer could take a good crack at it," I concluded.

"Mainstream religions have always insisted that the way to paradise is through a life without sin—through acts of compassion and love, even for your enemy. At least, that is what the Christian faith teaches—I couldn't really vouch for other religions."

"Let's stick to your Christian faith then—for the sake of this discussion," I replied. "It certainly emphasizes the idea that a person free of sins is headed for everlasting life in heaven—the only life that really matters."

"Yes! This also eases the pain in people with miserable lives—those living in poverty and filth. It provides them with something to look forward to—if they worship God and live a sinless life, of course."

"Good! But if such notions are true, the obvious way to reserve a seat next to the lord is by confessing your sins, receiving absolution, and then...killing yourself."

"But the Christian faith considers suicide a sin. The minute you commit it you are a sinner and you have no sure path to heaven."

"Singing the praises of heaven and then condemning someone who tries to get there any which way he can makes no logical sense—it is a giant contradiction. But I will let it go and concentrate on the following. What about cases where mothers kill their babies to save them from this evil world—as Christians enjoy calling it—and guarantee them a place in heaven? After all, who is more sinless than an infant, especially right after baptism? Of course, society pronounces such people *mentally disturbed* and locks them up, absolving religions of any moral responsibility. But if religions were honest about their pronouncements, shouldn't they be congratulating such people for discovering a sure path to heaven for their children—the only place to be?"

Estelle fell silent for a minute.

"What about mothers killing their children to save them from…satan? Does the church feel responsible for such crimes considering that satan is one of their creations?"

Estelle continued to remain silent.

"This was a good exchange—I better go write all these things down before I forget them," I muttered.

"Yeah, right! It's just more stuff for *intellectual masturbation*, that's all it is to you," she uttered straining to hide her internal rage.

I didn't respond. Sometimes the best answer is to say nothing.

Cause And Effect

"How can you see all this," Theodore pointed to some breath-taking scenery on a drive through a mountainous region of upper Georgia, "and claim that there is no God? What happened to your scientific argument of *cause and effect*—if something exists, someone or something created it? What about this beautiful lake, the mountains, the flowers and the trees, the divine harmony that exists around us?"

"What divine harmony?" I asked absent-minded, enjoying a peacefully bucolic scene in the valley below.

"The one that engulfs our lives. Don't you agree that our universe forms a harmonious whole? The sun that never fails to come up, the moon, the four seasons that rotate like clockwork, the delicate balance between plants and animals in one marvelous ecosystem—none of those move you to accept the harmony of this universe? Who could have created it, if not a powerful and benevolent God?"

Theodore is a family friend—a recent graduate of a theology school. He had accumulated loads of arguing ammunition from his classes in theology, philosophy, ethics and the like.

He was sneakily advancing the *cause and effect* argument, proposed as a proof of god's existence by some religious philosopher like Thomas Aquinas, Santayanna or Francis of Assisi. This argument—considered one of the so-called *cosmological* arguments [38]— is popular with people of the cloth, especially the part about the divine harmony that exists in the universe.

"What about the hurricanes, the earthquakes, the tsunamis, the droughts, the cataclysms, the famines, the massacres, the holocausts and the like? Do we put our head in the sand when they come up and spoil your so-called divine harmony?"

"There is the difference between believers and non-believers," he retorted. "We look for the beauty around us and thank God—you seek the ugly and painful so you can blame Him. I could tell you, of course, that the things you mentioned are the work of the Devil, but it wouldn't make much difference—you don't believe in him, either."

"There you go again—the same old song. Anything good cometh of god, anything bad of the devil—a win-win situation."

"All right, you made your point. But what about the *cause and effect* argument? You are not trying to weasel out of discussing it, are you? I am doing you a favor bringing it up—it's right down your scientific alley. I feel generous today—accommodating," he added, smiling.

"I certainly accept that since our universe exists, something has caused it," I replied. That is the scientific *cause and effect* principle that you are referring to. A pure accident could have brought it about, though, and that would satisfy the principle. But I would accept that some god made it, if you would consider the following question. If a god made it, then he exists. Who made him?"

"God is omnipotent. He exists—period."

"But you have agreed to the *cause and effect* principle. If he exists, someone created him. Who?"

Theodore kept staring at me, so I continued.

"The only acceptable answer is some other god—more powerful than the one you believe in. And if we accept that he exists, who created him? The principle obviously leads to a never-ending chain of gods, each stronger than the one before—all watching over this universe demanding that we worship them. You end up with more gods than the ancient Greeks—and the one you believe in, is the lowest one on the totem pole."

"You are simply irredeemable, and you force me to play the same game. OK, God created this universe, and there is no other God but him, because he came about by accident. Are you happy now? Does that satisfy all your moronic theories?"

"It sure does," I answered. "But an accident creating a god is tough to swallow. Certainly tougher than the Big Bang theory [50, 53, 54]."

"I've heard you admit that you haven't read the Big Bang theory all the way through—that it was too hard to understand it. How can you now accept it over a religious explanation that is self-evident? I suppose the next thing you will tell me is that you also believe that the start of life was some accident that produced a protoplasm [51-

52]."

"Look here," I replied. "I don't believe, nor do I blindly accept anyone's answers. I do confess, though, that between the two, I prefer science's answers to yours. Do you want to know why?"

"Why?" he shouted. "To infuriate me, right?"

"For one thing they are more mature, studied and sophisticated, while yours are naïve and adolescent—an affront to my intelligence. But the chief reason is that the scientists who proposed them never asked anyone to *worship* the Big Bang or the accident. They just suggested them as a plausible explanation. And if someone asks some questions, they listen and try to answer them—they don't condemn him to eternal damnation for asking them."

Good vs. Evil

"Answer me this if you can," Theodore said one late afternoon, as we are sitting in our back yard, sipping homemade limeade and enjoying the view of the lake. "How do you decide *good and evil* without the institution of the church? How do you entice people to follow a pious path without the fear of hell and the reward of heaven? How can you live without the ten commandments?"

"Not bad, not bad," I replied. "But if you have *good and evil* under control, why do we still need the law? How come the prisons are bursting at the seams with criminals? People haven't stopped criminal activities even when the penalty is their own lives and you think you are convincing them to abandon sinning?"

"Yes, I do. Even if religions have not totally stopped evil, they have reduced it—people are at least more civil to each other."

"Religions are redundant, if you want my opinion," I said. "Some, with their notion of confession and forgiveness, may even be responsible for at least a part of all this mayhem."

"What are you talking about? That is a low blow, totally unbecoming of you," he said, looking somewhat disturbed.

"I am talking about religions who use the concept of confession and routinely forgive serious crimes, wiping the slate clean," I replied. "Doesn't that encourage the criminal to a repeat performance? I tell you, it's the law that puts the...fear of god in them," I said laughing.

"Have you ever looked at a list of professions?" I asked him suddenly.

"Professions? What sort of professions are you talking about?

"Professions, occupations—the kinds of things that people do to earn a living."

"How is that related to our discussion here?" He was getting annoyed—just the way I wanted it.

"Well, start looking and you'll discover that most of the population is engaged in the *sin and crime area*. That's how much heed people are paying to your ten commandments. Do you want me to name a few of these professions?"

"Go ahead!"

"OK. Besides the criminals themselves, lawyers, police officers, FBI and CIA and INS agents, judges, parole officers, justice system employees, psychologists and psychiatrists, social workers, *grief counselors* (new gimmick), private eyes, bouncers, night watchmen, manufacturers of security devices and their employees, workers in hot lines for all sorts of crimes, insurance fraud investigators, prostitutes, drug pushers, bookies, sexual harassment ombudsmen or ombudswomen, spies, missile and spy equipment manufacturers, weapons manufacturers and their employees, mercenaries, terrorists, volunteer armies, collection agents, etc. And don't forget the thousands of priests, ministers, spiritualists and other such tireless referees of people's quarrels and disagreements "

"There is no way that those amount for more than half of the population."

"I am not finished. I just stopped to catch my breath," I replied. "The above are involved *full-time* in activities dealing with criminals. We also have millions of others who work part-time in the field. Those are the legislators and all associated civil servants, IRS and their agents, local and state government employees, personnel officers, managers…"

"Managers?"

"You bet! When I was chairing the department at the University, part of my time was spent in resolving problems between members of the faculty. You'd be shocked if you knew how routinely people try to…*screw* each other—how seldom they are willing to compromise when problems arise. I suspect that most managers—millions of people—spend part of their time just solving disputes among their perpetually bickering employees, like I did."

"And your final point is?" he asked anxiously.

"That people totally ignore the definitions of good and evil given by religions. Hell doesn't scare them enough—nobody remembers the ten commandments anymore. And we are not that civil to each other because of some religion, that's for sure. Societies understand this, and that is why they have laws, the police, courts and prisons, and managers. In short, religions are redundant—I told you this at the start of our discussion. Their contribution toward making people

34

behave is zilch, zero, a negative number—period."

His eyes took a glassy look and he stared at the sky.

"And you know something else?" I asked, pretending to be concerned. "You are becoming redundant as well—holding on to outdated concepts like *heaven and hell.* You've got to wake up and realize that the life of a priest is pointless, that...."

I had to stop because Theodore got up—his face red with anger—looking like a grenade with its string pulled.

"You went over the line," he shouted. "I am going to get you for this—you'll see."

"There you go," I replied. "See how impossible it is *to turn the other cheek?*"

His face twisted with the realization that he had fallen for my simple trick. He collapsed back into his chair and remained there pensive and embarrassed for quite some time. I harbored no illusions, of course, that I had converted him to my position. He was depressed because he had lost the argument. He had to rework his approach—open up a new angle.

But I wouldn't let him. The best defense is a good offense, I thought to myself, so I'd better get ready for our next meeting.

And I was.

A Loving And Forgiving God

"You use a lot of attributes when you describe your god," I started, "and some of them are often contradictory. The ones I am most miffed about are *loving, compassionate and forgiving*. How can you attribute such traits to a god who sends down calamities to those he dislikes? He even maintains a private torture chamber for the black-listed hardcore cases."

Theodore and I had just returned from a bike ride, having a cup of coffee on his verandah overlooking a river. I was somewhat irritated by the taste of his coffee—it was instant—and I took it out on his god.

"What torture chamber? Boy, you sure started out aggressively today," he remarked.

"I guess in your circles you call it hell."

"Hell is a torture chamber?"

"What do you call a place where people are placed in barrels full of hot oil, where vipers are commonplace and everyone is suffering unbearable pain for all eternity? Torture chamber is a mild word for all that, I assure you."

"Those that God sends to Hell deserve to be there, and it's not a torture chamber. People in torture chambers are there until they confess. There is nothing to confess in Hell. God knows all, and once in Hell, you are there forever."

"Condemned forever—that really squares off well with the notion of a forgiving god," I replied. "Now let's look at how loving and compassionate he is."

"Surely," Theodore said.

"Explain to me please why my colleague, Gene A., died of leukemia the year before last. He was in his thirties, a brilliant scientist and a charismatic teacher, and left a widow and a baby boy who depended on him. How could your compassionate and loving god allow this to happen?"

"You force me to say things I don't want to say. It might sound as if I am badmouthing the dead," he replied.

"We are alone here—go ahead and speak out honestly. I won't

37

hold it against you."

"Well, OK. The answer is that God does punish people when they commit serious sins against him."

"He punishes people for sinning with death?"

"The concept of sin is an essential part of the dogma in most religions. It is not, as you intimate, incompatible with love. You love your children, yet you punish them sometimes."

"OK. I will accept the explanation that Gene was being punished for some terrible sin, even though I think the punishment points to a vengeful, not a loving and compassionate god. But what about his wife? Did she also commit a sin and is being punished for it? Her husband was taken away, and she is left….."

"She might have been in on the same sin he was committing," Theodore interrupted. "We have no way of knowing what God knows."

"What about their baby? He couldn't have been in on the sin—he was only two months old. Why was he left without a father?"

"Maybe God decided that the child is better off without such a father. Ours is not to know why when it comes to the actions of the Lord," Theodore answered, crossing himself. "Besides, this whole supposition could be all wrong. Gene could have been a paragon of piety for all we know, and he still could have died."

"Really? Why?"

"It is well known that God sometimes does this sort of thing to test people's belief in Him," he replied.

"He throws out catastrophes to sinners—because they sinned against him—and to non-sinners to test the strength of their allegiance? Maybe the only people he leaves alone are non-believers like me."

"I wouldn't be so sure of that," Theodore replied, moving away from me to ensure his safety. "He could strike you dead this very minute if He wanted."

"I am truly amazed at your image of a loving god who comes with all these issues. Don't you feel that you are in a *damned-if-you-do-and-damned-if-you-don't* situation?"

"How so?"

"It makes no difference whether you are a sinner or a model

believer—you could be struck down either way. And to make matters worse, you don't even know why—he never tells you either way."

"You got it! Being a true believer is not easy—you got to stay alert, keep praying to be spared," Theodore replied.

"I guess so. But I am still a bit confused about your explanation of tragedies—that they are either caused because people sinned or were being tested."

"I'll be more than happy to elaborate."

"OK. Let's take that earthquake in South America the other day—some 10,000 people dead, including pregnant women, babies, etc. Your god could have averted it—they were mostly Christians—but he chose not to. Were they all sinners—even the babies? Or was he punishing some and testing the rest in one grand and efficient fell swoop? And how can any one of them prove that he can pass the test if he is dead? Don't you find any of this contradictory or paradoxical?"

"Not at all. But I'll tell you what I really found amazing about that earthquake. Did you see the village where everyone was wiped out and every structure was leveled except this one Christian church?"

"He was only keen in protecting his own church?"

"Wasn't that an incredible miracle?" he asked.

"Hallelujah!" I replied.

Everyone Believes In Something

"I've got a good one for you, *a proof*—our professor called it—that God exists."

It was Jasmine, the University student from across the street. She caught me outside in the yard trimming the hedge on a balmy afternoon—springtime in the late 1980s. She was taking a course on *Religions of the World*, and she often stopped by to get my reaction to some of the issues.

"Fire away," I responded.

"The proof said that in every tribe, every nation, at every time during recorded history, people had some religion—they worshiped a God or Gods. That cannot be a mere coincidence, he said—it is *proof that God exists*. What do you think? Is it?"

"Well, it is also a historical fact that people always had some form of language, some form of music—art in general. Did some other gods introduce these things to prove that they exist? The ancient Greeks actually thought that this explanation is reasonable. They had gods for music, war, love, art, hunting, the ocean—all things of importance in their lives."

"So you don't think it is proof that God exists then?" Jasmine wanted to know.

"Nope," I said. "The fact that all known tribes had a religion only proves that *they all felt a need—a desire—to have one*. The professor's conclusion that this desire proves god's existence is not logical. It is not new either—it dates back to the Middle Ages."

"If it doesn't prove God's existence, what does it prove? Why did everyone have a religion?" she persisted. "It sounds fishy to me."

"I don't think we really know yet," I replied. "There are a couple of answers—besides the one served by your professor—but research is continuing on the issue."

"Could you please describe them? I am supposed to write a term paper on this, and I need an answer that will be noticed. I've got to get this guy's attention to pull in a good grade—the class is large."

"The most popular answer is based on man's perennial fear of the unknown," I started. "It is pretty obvious that all tribes were scared

41

of some unexplained object or phenomenon in their lives—lions, bulls, lightning, snakes, their ancestors, death, etc. So they dreamed up a god who caused it, and worshipped him to feel safe. Sometimes they actually worshipped the object or phenomenon itself—to pacify it. What object or phenomenon they worshiped or which god depended on the people, their location, their fears and their imagination. Since there are always things to fear, there is always religion. This answer is logically superior to the one that your professor suggested. He must be religious, by the way. His answer is routine among the faithful."

"And you are not, so your answers are preferred by the non-believers, right?"

"Obviously," I replied. "A second answer," I went on, "which is less known but more fascinating and quite controversial, is that we have evolved from some ape-like creature, and thus carry some of this ape's state of mind. Now, most apes live in small groups or *tribes* much like humans, and in these tribes, there is always a supreme leader. This No.1 ape—the Silverback in gorilla societies [61]—is a god to the other apes. He protects the troop, he keeps order, he demands blind obedience, and he gets it. This idea—that there is always some god, and he must be worshiped—is in all the brains of the ape subjects, because it keeps the troop united, harmonious and safe and serves their better survival. Well, if we are descendants of some such ape, it is reasonable to expect that we carry this same idea in our heads also. That just like our ape ancestors, we yearn for someone to worship as god. Quite likely it serves our better survival as well."

"That's amazing," Jasmine said. "An idea in our head that comes from our ape ancestors? I can see why religions would frown on that—might even chase you out of town! But if that is the reason, why don't people satisfy their need by declaring their leader—*their Silverback*—a God?"

"In many cases they do," I replied. "In some cases the leader himself senses this need and declares himself a god to satisfy it, serving his own selfish interests in the process. The Pharaohs did it, the Roman emperors did it, the Emperor of Ethiopia claimed it in recent times, and some—the Rastaferians [58]—still worship him in some islands of the Caribbean Sea. It is also noteworthy that in democracies where the leader never hangs around long enough to be deified, the citizens turn to organized religions with more fervor than they do in kingdoms or dictatorships. The idea that they must worship someone is always in them—and no king around to satisfy it. The whole notion is not that bizarre—it might be at least part of the reason why people always hungered for a deity. It also explains rather neatly why god is always described as an *iron-fisted* dictator—a benevolent egomaniac who keeps order and protects everyone in exchange for complete submission to his dictates."

"I kinda like it," Jasmine said. "When I was a little girl, I actually thought that the president of the United States was a God. I was disappointed when I was told that he was not—sort of like when I realized that Santa Claus didn't really exist."

"If you like it, go ahead and use it in your paper," I suggested. "Your professor will definitely notice it. Religious folk get infuriated—they *go ape*, as it were—when someone suggests that our behavior emulates some ape," I concluded, unable to stop myself from laughing.

Miracles

"I know that you don't believe in God, the creator, but what about Jesus Christ—our Savior?"

It was Mathias, the born-again Christian, my tennis partner at the University intramural games. He was a member of one of those evangelical groups who shouted "Jeeeesus" at every turn.

"What about him?" I asked.

"How can you deny His power? He performed miracles, didn't He? He cured the blind, He fed...."

"First of all, there isn't much historical evidence that Jesus ever existed as the person described in the gospels [10,59,60]. Even if he did, the actual execution of these miracles could be disputed as a figment of the evangelists' imagination, or they could have been faked [62,63]. But I am going to be munificent—call me a softie if you must, but that's the way I feel today—and grant you all that, so that we can concentrate on a debate on miracles. Do you feel that if someone can perform miracles he should be declared a god?"

"I certainly do," he said. "Who else but a God can perform them?"

"Well, Oral Roberts and Benny Hinn[6] can," I replied. "John the Baptist was performing miracles at the same time as Jesus, if I am not mistaken. Most of the saints of Catholicism have performed miracles—they must do two to be declared a saint. Even *statues* and *religious icons* have performed them. Are we to pronounce all these gods?"

Mathias looked contemplative for a while—a brief, fleeting moment of doubt on his face. He quickly regained his composure though, offering the following remark.

"I guess it always comes down to faith! Logical arguments will never swing anyone one way or the other. Personally, I am in awe of Jesus Christ's ability to perform miracles as He did and you are

---

[6] Oral Roberts and Benny Hinn performed miracles on US Television in the 60s and 90s, respectively.

totally unmoved by them. I don't know what he could have done to impress you and convince you of His deity."

"I'll tell you of one type of miracle he might have performed which would shake me up a bit—something that none of the miracle performers have ever even tried," I volunteered.

"And what would this miracle be that would impress your Highness?" he asked, sarcastically.

"The epitome of miracles would be the restoration to life of someone whose head was chopped off," I replied. "There would be no doubt—you can't fake it with a severed head, you know. In the absence of that, I would also be astonished if someone showed up with one leg, and a second leg was miraculously planted upon him. Even the restoration of a missing toe would be a fantastic feat—might drop me on my knees for a prayer. That's not asking much, is it?"

"These feats—even the missing toe—are impossible," Mathias protested.

"Isn't that what miracles are supposed to be?" I countered. "The ones usually performed are quite banal—easily faked. Even if they truly occurred, they can easily be attributed to the Placebo effect [64,65]."

"The Placebo effect? How so?"

"Up to 40% of people are cured of various diseases by swallowing a pill they believe to be a cure even though the pill is a sugar pill. The credit for such cures is given to the Placebo effect—in case you didn't know. For the Placebo effect to work, the person taking the sugar pill must *firmly believe that the pill will cure him*. That is why Jesus always demanded that the afflicted *totally and unequivocally believed in his power to cure them*—he wanted the Placebo effect to be on his side."

"So you found a way to trivialize even the miracles that Jesus Christ actually performed with this ridiculous Placebo effect of yours," he replied, staring at me as if he was witnessing the second coming of the devil. "I see a serious blasphemy in what you just spouted—calling the miracles *banal* and accusing Jesus of using the Placebo effect to his favor. You are also implying that he knew that he could not perform *real* miracles—that He knew that He was not the Son of God."

"I think you might be hard-pressed to find a place in the Bible, where Jesus claimed to be the *son of god,*" I replied. "All he ever declared was that he was the *son of man*—his father, Joseph, I presume."

"Besides," I added. "There is no blasphemy, if I don't believe in blasphemy."

He Died To Save Us!

"Let me take the aggressive side for a change and see how you make out defending your position," I told Mathias one sunny morning during one of our tennis breaks.

"Sure, go for it," Mathias replied, always eager to try for a convert.

"OK," I replied, "I am hereby submitting to you that most of your Christian phrases are gibberish—they are meaningless religious apothegms."

Mathias's face looked like I had just slapped it—twice.

"This you got to prove," he hissed. "I am not letting you off the hook this time. Would you be kind enough to give me a *for instance*?" he added sarcastically, regaining his composure.

"Most of the phrases used by your Christian leaders like *living in god's grace, born again, god is infinitely forgiving and compassionate* are void of any real meaning. When pressed to explain them, they go into a boring diatribe that sounds profound but clouds them even further."

"These concepts are very clear to all god-loving, god-fearing people," Mathias replied.

"There, you did it yourself," I interjected. "You used the word god-fearing trying to describe a religious virtue. Why should anyone fear your god if he is ever-loving and infinitely compassionate? Don't you see that all this is drivel? Catchy phrases, like the ones used in television commercials?"

"Very well," Mathias answered angrily. "Which of these phrases are you willing to debate? I am ready to show you that the phrases are loaded with religious meaning, and that it is you, who—being void of spirituality—is unable to comprehend them."

"Spirituality, you say. That is another word that can mean anything one desires. But never mind that—let's zero in on our debate. Let's look at the phrase—one of my favorites—*Jesus died to save us*. Evangelists get lots of mileage out of that one—it gives the audience a sense of guilt, and softens them up for the rest of the fatuous shibboleths that they spout, not to mention the collection plate."

"You even find that phrase offensive?" he mused. "That God sacrificed his son to save us from our sins? That is one of the cornerstones of our Christian faith."

"Then it should be easy for you to explain it to me," I replied.

"What bothers you about the phrase?" Mathias asked cockily. "Jesus died on the cross to cleanse us of our sins. That is a huge sacrifice and we should all be thankful for it. And not only to Him, but to God as well—for sacrificing His son to save us."

"Here's my first question," I replied. "To begin with, why is it a sacrifice? Life here on this earth—according to Christians—is not as important, or even as pleasant as it is in heaven. Jesus knew in advance that he was going to heaven—to a prominent place next to his father's throne in paradise. All he did was speed up his ascension to this attractive and desirable place. And all that god did was get his son back from this miserable place called earth. Where is the sacrifice in any of this? It was all a self-serving grand theatrical performance to show the audience that he was the son of god. I would have done the same in a jiffy, if I were he. The idea that it was a sacrifice is not only preposterous; it is actually demeaning to him."

"Demeaning?" Mathias gasped.

"Yeah, demeaning. He is, presumably, the son of god—a god himself, for chrissake. He could die anyway he wants—without any pain if he so desires. In fact, according to your bible, after his death, he actually returned to earth and chatted with his apostles by and by. And if we accept that he is omnipotent, he can re-die every which way he chooses and return to the planet as he sees fit. He can appear to be suffering while he is having a jolly old good time. He may even be doing that a lot, for all you know. This might be his job, so to speak. To say that while he is doing his job, he is in pain and thus sacrificing himself is to belittle his powers, to make him appear less than a god. I don't think he is looking down kindly on those who utter such insulting phrases," I added.

"I don't often…"

"But ridiculous as this notion of the sacrifice might be, it is not the main reason why this phrase is complete hogwash," I interrupted him.

"Oh, really?" Mathias replied somewhat pensively. "What is it then?"

"It is the other half of the phrase, this business of *saving us* that is the real mumbo-jumbo," I replied.

"How so?"

"What did he save us from?" I asked him.

"Well, from our sins," Mathias replied triumphantly, confident that this time he had the right cliché.

"All our sins—past, present and future?"

"Yes."

"If that is so, does it mean that every time we sin now, we are automatically forgiven because he died on the cross? Does it mean that we have a license to violate all the commandments—even to kill—because we have been already saved, and our future actions are pre-forgiven? That no matter what we do from here on, we are all headed for paradise?"

"I don't think so," Mathias replied. "Otherwise we would not be talking about our sins now—we wouldn't be needing to confess them asking for absolution."

"Precisely," I replied. "Christian religions continue to teach that people are still sinners. Catholic, Eastern Orthodox and many other dogmas demand that all newborns be baptized so that they are cleared of the original sin [66,67]—we weren't even saved from that, it appears. So what did Jesus save us from when he died on the cross?"

"I may no longer know the answer to that question," Mathias replied, eyes directed towards the ground with consternation, "but I am quite certain of this. People that don't believe in Jesus *are not saved*. Ponder that for the rest of your godless life."

51

The Mother Of All Scams

"So what do you think?" I asked Akis H., a longtime friend from the time of undergraduate days at the University of Minnesota. "Do you care to critique the manuscript at this point, or do you need time to absorb the arguments?"

"I think I can do it now," he replied. "Many of these arguments are not new to me—I've heard you using them before during some of our old discussions. They are a bit more polished now—a bit more mature and logically sound—but the tone has remained the same. I dare say you don't seem to have mellowed much over the years."

We had just completed a refreshing swim in the blue sparkling waters of the Mediterranean Sea at Kyllini, on the western side of the Peloponese Island in Greece. It was late afternoon, and the waiter was bringing us two cups of that black, thick liquid that masquerades as coffee in most parts of the country. It was called Turkish coffee in the past, but it has been recently baptized as *Byzantine*, for obvious reasons.

He had just finished reading the first part of the manuscript—the material up to the present dialogue—and I was interested in his reaction. Akis shared my views on religion, so I didn't expect any serious objections to the contents—just some critiquing of the tone and style.

"So you think I am too harsh on religions and the faithful?" I asked him.

"Well, I am reminded of Alfred Hitchcock's deathbed statement," Akis remarked while fidgeting with the utensils trying to add more sugar to his already syrupy drink.

"How come? How does it relate to our conversation?"

"He was asked if he learned anything from a lifetime of directing scary movies—anything that helped him make his movies even scarier. Do you know what he replied?"

"No."

"That he learned that *people will listen to anything you say, as long as you* whisper *it to them.*"

53

"So what are you implying?"

"That you are shouting in this chapter—not whispering. You might want to tone down the stridency. Most religious people will dismiss these dialogues as smart-alecky exhibitions of obnoxious wit and toss them aside."

His comments were not surprising. Akis is a mild-mannered fellow who constantly worries about *political correctness*—about unwittingly insulting his fellow man.

"I actually did make a serious effort to tone it down," I replied, gazing at the shadowy, mountainous shoreline of the island of Zakynthos in the horizon. "But if it doesn't show, I might just as well go all the way and express my true feelings about religions. Holding back was dishonest, anyway."

"Oh, yeah, there is more?" Akis replied with mild interest in his voice. "Why don't you just tell me first to see how it plays out? You can decide whether you want to include it or not, at a later time. This coffee has awakened every gram of my aging brain and only a sharp sequence of outrageous ideas will pacify it now."

"OK, here it goes synoptically," I said. "Religion is the mother of all scams—the biggest, longest running con game ever devised by humans on this planet. And since the perpetuators of the scan enjoy a respected, highly privileged place in society, I hereby pronounce this scam as the most successful one ever."

"Oh, I love it," Akis replied popping his eyes wide open. "Can you elaborate on it further? Do you mean a scam like selling *snake-oil* at the circus?"

"Precisely, though in a much grander scale," I replied. "What does the seller of snake-oil claim about his product? That if you buy it and drink it regularly, it will cure all diseases—biological or mental. Does he have any proof for his claims? None, though he will parade many people who swear that they drank it and it worked. And what happens to such merciless merchants of false hope, if they are reported to the authorities? They are locked up in jail—that's what."

Akis was staring at me now—his eyes begging me to continue.

"Now, let us turn to the sellers of religion. To begin with, they have no risk and no expenses—they don't even bother to include a bottle with some colored liquid in it. What they sell—and you pay dearly for it to support their lavish lifestyle—is air, words, empty promises. Join them, they say, and belief in god and perpetual praying will fulfill all your needs, dreams and expectations in this life and the one right after. They promise the same stuff as the snake-oil merchants and more—they promise happiness, everlasting bliss, and eternal life in heaven. And all this for a mere 10% of your earnings and half of your waking hours."

"Now that you mentioned it, it is kind of unbelievable," Akis volunteered.

"Just wait—I am not finished yet," I replied. "We all know that the snake-oil salesman vanishes from view to avoid complaints about his product. Right?"

"Right."

"Well, do the peddlers of religion ever disappear to avoid complaints? On the contrary, they live opulent and ostentatious lives. What of their extravagant houses, their jewelry, their velvet capes, golden scepters, jewel-studded headgear and the like? What about their fancy cars, trips to exotic places, lavish structures they call church complexes but which are really their office quarters? The scammers exhibit a standard of living a thousand fold above that of the scammed."

"All with money that the faithful pay for a non-existent return," Akis added.

"Exactly. Do you recall the well-known TV evangelist with the air-conditioned doghouse[7]? What about the eastern type *gurus?* One of them—Maharishi something or other—lived in eastern Oregon with his followers and with 19 Cadillacs for his riding pleasure. And the scam goes on."

"Are they ever arrested by the authorities for the scam?" Akis wondered.

"Arrested? Never in your life," I replied. "The scam is not against the law. Besides, in most places the authorities are part of it."

Akis was getting agitated now, his eyes rapidly losing their

---

[7] Jim Bakker, who was imprisoned in the 1990s for real estate fraud.

peaceful gaze.

"In other words," I went on, "these are no ordinary nickel-and-dime vagabonds—they are the kings of scam. They have a masterfully designed and brilliantly executed scheme with pre-patented answers for all eventualities. It is totally guaranteed."

"What do you mean by pre-patented answers?" Akis demanded to know.

"Well, let me run you through a typical execution of their scam," I replied. "Let's say you joined, and at some point in your life you are diagnosed with cancer. If you ask them whether you should go through the recommended medical therapy most religions will say yes. But continued worship of the lord and chronic praying is important for a favorable outcome of the medical therapy, they will advise."

"I guess that is one of their patented answers. But why should that be so? Why can't god cure you without the drugs? Is he invested in some drug company for his pension?" Akis had started to get in on the act now—his eyes indicating eerie satisfaction.

"You tell me," I replied smiling. "Now let us assume that therapy, perpetual worshipping and praying fails and the cancer marches on with vigor. Do you know what their patented answer is?"

"Yes, I do," Akis replied. "That you still did not pray hard enough, or that your faith might have momentarily wavered, or some other cliché like *the Lord works in mysterious ways and yours is not to ask why but just to believe*."

"Precisely. These are all *textbook* answers, known to sit well with the faithful. I tell you, these guys are so confident of their con game that they don't even try to avoid a confrontation—they stare you down with arrogance, putting the blame squarely on your shoulders."

"It is incredible," Akis replied with fire in his eyes. I was witnessing a strange metamorphosis of a mild mannered chap into an angry tiger.

"Now let us assume that the disease brings you down to your knees and you are on your deathbed, still wondering why god in his mysterious ways has singled you out for death rather than cure. Well, now their patented answer is that either you are being punished for sinning, or that you were one of the chosen few to be rushed to god's side—that he is freeing you from this evil world. I tell you, man, they have a Ph.D in the theory of con games."

Akis now appeared to be working himself into a frenzy.

"That is outrageous," he cried. "They have a fool-proof scam, airtight from all angles. They are untouchable."

"You bet," I agreed. "And now let me give you their scam's final masterful stroke. Let's say that you are one of the rare few that keep demanding satisfaction—keep pestering them with questions that raise doubts about their doctrines. Do you know what they do then?"

"What?"

"They deliver their coup de grace—*excommunication.* This means expulsion from the Church and condemnation to eternal hell with no possibility of parole. Such punishment is normally god's prerogative during judgment day. But if you commit the ultimate crime of insulting them, they declare…Marshall Law and take over god's duties with unprecedented audacity. I tell you, if all this isn't the zenith of swindles, the epitome of rip-offs, I don't know what is. No wonder it has lasted for 10,000 years with no sign of abating. And if you think that they would be happy with all that, you are sadly mistaken. They have even asked, and they have received a *tax-exempt status.*"

Akis was out of his chair now, looking like a wild man—an animal. I think I saw a trace of froth at the corners of his mouth.

"They are despicable scoundrels, leeches, rogues," he shouted. "Look man, I am sorry about what I said at the start. Your dialogues are not strident—they are wimpy, if anything. Now that I see through their deception so clearly, I almost wish there was a god up there to stick it to them, even if only in the afterlife. They sure aren't going to get their due here in this world and they know it."

"So now you think that the book is too placid?" I asked faking astonishment. "In that case, I'll just include this here conversation. That ought to fix the problem."

And Man Created God

"It appears to me (whether rightly or wrongly) that direct arguments against Christianity and theism produce hardly any effect on the public."

Charles Darwin

It took Akis two more cups of that coffee and a long swim in the calm Mediterranean waters before he regained his composure and became able to resume our conversation. By then it was time to return home. My wife, Estelle, was expecting us for late afternoon tea.

"You know," he finally said as we were getting into the car, "there is a serious question here that demands an answer. Maybe you can come up with one and include it in your book."

"What's the question?" I asked.

"Why do people need religion so badly that that don't mind being scammed?"

I glanced briefly at Akis, quickly returning my eyes back to the road. The traffic was heavy and the road back to Patras was narrow.

"Now you are touching upon one of the great mysteries of human behavior—religiosity," I replied. "There are a number of other serious questions concerning this issue that we should raise before making a concerted stab at the answers."

"Like what?" Akis wondered.

"Well, you have probably noticed that there are three principal groups of people—the religious, the doubters and the non-believers. In between these three, there exist myriads of shades—the spectrum of religiosity appears to be continuous. Are you with me so far?"

"Yes."

"OK. Have you also noticed that deeply religious people ignore arguments that show the absurdity of their beliefs? Some—the fanatics—become outraged at the suggestion that religions are illogical or unnecessary, or at hints that other religions may be better than theirs."

"It sounds like you have had some frustrating experiences with

59

the deeply devout," Akis remarked frowning.

"Frustrating is a mild word," I replied. "I am confessing right here and now that despite a plethora of religious verbal clashes, at no instance did I ever convert a *profound* believer to a non-believer. My most brilliant demonstration of the illogicality of his convictions was always delivered in vain."

"Gee, I am sorry, man," Akis replied. "I had sensed a grudge on your part, but..."

"No, you are wrong," I interrupted him. "I have no grudge against the highly religious—no grudge at all. The fact is they hold no monopoly in this type of behavior. Haven't you noticed that the non-believers are also tightly cemented to their views? That they view the faithful with *mocking hostility*, hinting that their IQ is less then adequate? I think I have to admit here as well, that proselytizing non-believers is a waste of time. They, too, with rare exceptions stay non-believers throughout their lifetimes."

"Now that you mentioned it, yes, I have observed it also," Akis responded.

"And what about the group in between these two—the doubters?" I continued. "Why are they moving in and out of some faith with interludes of rebellious faithlessness? Can you explain this type of behavior?"

"I certainly can't," Akis replied. "But I don't have to—I am not the one writing the book."

"There are other intriguing questions," I continued. "Are you willing to listen to some more of them while we are driving home?"

"Only if you promise to come up with some answers at the end," Akis replied.

"OK. I promise," I said. "But since the answers might turn scholarly, it might require some of the references that I have at home. You'll have to wait till we get there."

"No problem. I am ready for the questions," he said sinking into the passenger seat while pushing the proper knob to lower the backrest.

"All right then. Here's one. Have you noticed that some, who appear indifferent to religion, drop down on their knees and pray at the first signs of danger or when death is imminent? What's up with them?"

"I usually hold such people in contempt," Akis volunteered. "At the same time I cringe at the thought that something like that might happen to me someday—maybe on my deathbed."

"Here's another one," I continued. "Why are some people willing to massacre innocents and even sacrifice their own life in the name of their god or their religion? The Crusades, the conflict in Northern Ireland and the bombing of the World Trade Center in New York in 2001 are vivid illustrations of this type of behavior." Akis had actually closed his eyes now, but I kept going. I enunciated each question slowly and clearly, pausing between questions to allow him to absorb their meaning thoroughly.

"During horrendous catastrophes (earthquakes, hurricanes, acts of terrorism, etc), thousands of innocents often die unfathomable deaths. Despite the obvious incompatibility of the carnage with the image of a just and compassionate god, people's faith is actually strengthened."

"All peoples throughout recorded history have had some religion as part of their culture. Why? This question was examined earlier in this book[8], but no definitive answer was given."

"Why is it that during a war both sides claim to have god on their side? How can each side claim that *good is fighting evil*, with evil always being on the other side?"

"Why do people tolerate oppressive theocratic regimes? Even in democracies you often see some tireless defenders of personal freedoms—paragons of democratic ideals and principles—rushing to join churches organized and run like the worst kinds of *banana republics*. Why?"

This last question coincided with the end of the drive, and I pulled the car into the garage. Akis opened his eyes and made as if he had been listening right along. I didn't really care whether he had heard all the questions or not. I just outlined them here for the sake of the book reader.

---

[8] See the dialogue entitled *Everyone Believes in Something* in Chapter 1.

Presently we got out of the car, climbed the stairs to the entry porch and marched straight to the office.

Akis stretched out in a comfortable chair and rested his legs on the coffee table.

"So, I'm ready for the answers. Have you got a theory that can explain all these things in a unified way?"

"There may be several that could do it, but I am going to give you my favorite one here—the one that I developed myself," I replied. "Have you read my other book, the one I wrote under the pseudonym of Aris P. D'Avenal [1]?"

"Yes, I have," Akis replied. "That's where you theorized that all our personality traits (from conservatism to jealousy, from lying to patriotism, even dancing) are caused by genes in our DNA. You called it the GSP theory—Genes and the Survival Principle—if I remember right. Oh, I get it now! It is that Gene of Religiosity you mentioned there that's causing all this bizarre religious behavior. Right?"

"Absolutely right," I replied. "For matters of faith, the theory of human behavior proposed there maintains that humans are born with a *Gene of Religiosity (GOR). This gene pre-programs our brain to believe in a superior being—a god—and* this belief leads smoothly to the development of organized religions. This GOR and a couple more concepts can explain pretty much everything."

"What concepts?" Akis wondered.

"One of them is that the GOR—like all genes—can have a variable strength in each of us depending on hereditary and environmental factors. The range of values is continuous but for the sake of simplicity we will assume it here to be on a scale from zero to ten. Your GOR strength and mine are probably somewhere around zero."

"Mine is totally defective—dead," Akis said laughing loudly. "But I guess most people must have a GOR strength from four to six—in the middle of the range, right?"

"Yes," I replied. "They are religious, but not fanatically so. They believe in god, they belong to a church and they participate in its religious activities. Such people are in the majority in most societies."

"What about people with GOR strength of 7-10? Are they the zealots, the fanatics, the perpetual proselytizers?"

"Exactly. Especially those in the upper part of this range."

"Their behavior is so very hard to fathom."

"It may be perplexing to the uninitiated, but it's really textbook to students of the GSP. If your GOR strength is that high, you are at this gene's mercy. You must proselytize, you must ensure that all followers are in line and if you detect emerging dissent, you must eliminate it."

"That is scary."

"And it gets scarier. Do you recall that under the GSP theory, a concept of paramount importance is the *genal condition*?"

"I think I do," Akis replied scratching his head. "Is that the notion that when someone feels threatened, his GOR strength jumps higher and higher until his brain converts him to an automaton—a zombie?"

"Something like that," I said laughing. "When the perceived danger is great, the rise in the strength of the GOR is substantial, and the individual goes in the so-called *genal condition*, a state where reason is absent and behavior is automatic. This state, blueprinted by the GOR, is also postulated as a pre-wired brain response."

"If that is true, then even mildly religious people can become fanatics," Akis suggested.

"They can and they do," I replied. "History has recorded many instances where groups of ordinary people commit revolting crimes under a religious *genal* condition. When the perceived danger is removed, they are amazed at their previous behavior."

"That explains a lot of puzzling religious atrocities. But what happens to people with high GOR strength, when they are placed in the genal condition? Does their strength go higher than 10?"

"It looks like it—it seems to run off the charts. They are placed in some *super-genal* condition metamorphosing into religious berserkers. They are the ones that commit the most diabolically heinous crimes, all the while convinced that they are serving their almighty. It is such people that committed the suicide attacks on New York's World Trade Center in 2001, and daily sacrifice themselves during suicide bombings in the Middle Eastern conflict. A charismatic leader can easily place them in this *super-genal* condition by suggesting a real or imaginary threat to their religion. I tell you, it's amazing, but the GOR can explain even the weirdest quirk of human religious behavior."

"I like it," Akis responded.

"Now a GOR strength of around 2 or 3 explains the doubters. Under normal living conditions they are either indifferent to religion or *declared* infidels. But in the face of real or perceived imminent danger—especially death—the strength could jump to 5 or 6, converting them temporarily to believers. If they die after the conversion and they are celebrities, they become pawns in the religious propaganda. But if they do not die and their *genal* condition eases, they usually return to their doubting selves. It all fits in quite nicely as you can see."

"What about those with really low values of zero to two?"

"They are the non-believers. In western societies they are treated with some contempt—in large cities with benign neglect. In most other societies they are in the closet, afraid that their careers might be ruined and their families stigmatized. In theocratic countries, they are imprisoned or executed."

"But why did nature put this gene in us?" Akis wondered. "I seem to remember from your GSP theory that if we have a gene, it's there to serve our good survival."

"Religion serves survival by being part of the culture. Culture, in turn, serves survival as the adhesive that bonds the tribe together. Many peoples came close to extinction but survived because of the strength of their culture—that is how important culture is. By the way, the idea that religion serves survival is also acknowledged by others [27]."

Just then my wife, Estelle, entered the office bringing espresso coffee and a stack of cookies in a large tray. I have already mentioned that she is rather unhappy about the book—her GOR is around six.

"You two guys—a mutual admiration society—can sit and criticize religions all you want. In the meantime, the people keep flocking to the parish churches."

"The reason for that is the GOR."

"A gene sends them there?"

"The GOR behaves similarly to the gene of hunger; it creates the appetite and people are compelled to seek food. Just like with sex. No gene whispers in your ear to look for a brothel but…"

"I don't think these similes are appropriate," Estelle interrupted. "I know you like them because they shock. But they are not convincing and they are insulting."

"How about the need for love? Or the need for language?"

"Can I ask you just one question?"

I sensed trouble, but I had to agree.

"Assuming that this gene exists and is needed for survival, wouldn't people like you two be *abnormal*? You have admitted that your GOR strength is so low, your gene might be kaput."

A low blow but she was capable of it. Akis, quite familiar with Estelle's bluntness, looked amused.

"Maybe so. But we no longer call people who deviate from the norm abnormal. We now call them *special*." I laughed.

"So you admit that you are abnormal—special, whatever?"

"We would be seriously abnormal in a society for which these genes evolved—the hunter/gatherer type. There was only one religion then, and it united the tribe into a strong, cohesive unit. We now live in an era during which the multi-ethnic/multi-cultural societies are becoming the norm and religion can no longer serve its original purpose. Under some circumstances—a war with religious undertones, for example—it could easily become a divisive rather than a unifying force."

"All of which makes us a new breed of super-people, perfectly suited for this brave new world," Akis added his cliché with a wide smile.

He had sunk deeper into his chaise lounge by now—arms stretched behind his back. He looked like he was watching a stage play—"*Who is Afraid of Virginia Wolff*" or something.

"Are you happy with the answer to your question?" I asked Estelle somewhat sarcastically.

"Oh, yes—overjoyed," she replied. "Let me see. First you humbly admit that you are abnormal. Then you turn it around and start calling yourself a new breed, demoting religion to a dying institution. Why I even serve you guys coffee—I'll never know."

"Maybe you've got a strong *gene of hospitality?*" Akis butted in innocently.

"Now you did it!" Estelle burst out. "Let me tell you two. There is no evidence that there is any GOR, anyway. All this stuff is all Nico's—she calls me Nico—speculation. I didn't want to emphasize this before, but since..."

"Maybe there wasn't any evidence when I first proposed it, but there is now," I interrupted.

"What?"

"I wasn't planning to elaborate—scholarship is not the main focus of this book—but since you are attacking my life's work, I must defend it appropriately," I said smiling.

"Go ahead—I am quite interested in this myself," Akis interjected with curiosity.

"OK. I believe Aris P. D'Avenal [1] is the first to put forth the hypothesis that genes in our DNA dictate all aspects of our personality. In formulating this hypothesis he was, of course, influenced by other present day thinkers and researchers [6,8]. For the religiosity gene in particular, there appears to be quite a multitude of researchers [2,3,4,5,7,13,27,56,57] who agree that religiosity is biologically derived."

"I don't care what they agree on," Estelle interrupted. "Do they have any evidence?"

"I was just getting to that. The best indication that religiosity is pre-wired in our brains comes from research at the University of California, San Diego and the University of North Carolina, where studies show that epilepsy and hallucinogenic drugs can easily produce *religious epiphanies* in people. At Laurentian University in Canada, when people are outfitted with a specially designed magnetized helmet, four out of five report spiritual experiences that involve god, demons or evil spirits. You can read a review and commentary of all these researches in reference 3, with details in 2, 4, and 5. In conclusion, scientific evidence that religiosity is biologically driven is mounting, and the hypothesis is rapidly gaining widespread acceptance."

Estelle looked somewhat stunned.

"Really?" said Akis. "That means that we have proof that *god is a creation of the human mind*—that he does not really exist." Then turning to Estelle, "This must be shocking to you—what with all the time you spend in the church and all."

"Shocking? Do you think that evidence by a bunch of pointed-headed scientists is going to shake my faith? A year ago, Nico told me that my love for our children was pre-programmed in my brain. Did I stop loving them? Last week he told Edna—my friend—that her passion for fishing was caused by a strong *fishing gene*. Well, I saw Edna yesterday and she was juggling her schedule to double her fishing trips. And, by the way, both of you have often declared that sex is all in your heads. I haven't noticed any change in your behavior—not in Nico's, anyway."

"Look here," I said, standing up and taking on a dapper professorial air. "Let's quit all these polemics and seek peace between the two camps. This should be the result of the GSP theory, anyway."

"Really? How so? A minute ago the GSP was responsible for equating churches to brothels. How is it now a peace offering?"

"Because among other things, it underscores the fact that *we all are what we are, and there is nothing we can do about it*—we have no choice in the matter."

"I guess considering your assaults on faith throughout this book, this does look like a peace offering," Estelle remarked with a hint of a smile.

"There is also another reason why peace is possible. Since our religiosity is fixed, we pose no threat to each other—the genal condition is unnecessary. Our two camps can discuss things with calm and reason."

Estelle picked up the dishes, put them in a tray and left without a word. She seemed pleased with this final outcome.

"Personally I think the evidence is strong—religion is finished," Akis remarked. "I am sure you agree but did not want to stress it during Estelle's presence."

I looked at him thoughtfully

"Sorry to disappoint you but I agree with Estelle," I surprised him. "Religious behavior will not change, not unless some selective cataclysm takes place which wipes all the religious people out while it leaves the freethinkers unscathed. But that would require a miracle, and here we don't believe in miracles."

"Well, there is still a chance that the believers will destroy themselves—they've been at each other for thousands of years. Unless this GSP theory bridges the gap between them."

"Not a chance," I replied. "Their gap is a giant chasm. The GSP is good, but not that good."

Play It Safe!

Let me end with a typical conversation between a non-believer and a doubter. The doubter in this case was Abe, a Jewish neighbor. Our family lived on the first floor of a large house in Medford, Massachusetts, and Abe and his family on the second. The period was late nineteen sixties. Abe practiced his religion without much conviction—with very little enthusiasm. Yet he refused to give it up altogether.

"The way I see it," he said one day stretched out in a chair, sipping some of my Metaxa brandy, "you've got to play it safe. Maybe there is a God, and maybe there isn't. I don't really know for sure—maybe nobody does. But are you willing to take the chance that there isn't, then suffer the consequences if there is? I am not—too chicken for that. So, I go around telling myself that he exists—I play it safe. That is the best argument I can come up with for believing. It has put enough fear in me to entice me to— more or less—practice my religion."

"Hold your horses—don't count your blessings yet," I retorted. "If there is an almighty out there, he *knows* what you are doing. He knows that you are not a believer at heart—just a pretender and a hypocrite. He just heard you say it—*you are playing* it *safe*. I would rather admit that I am a non-believer, and take my chances as an honest man."

"Wait, I didn't mean it that way," he said apologetically, looking up toward the ceiling. "What I meant was that when I have doubts, I put them out of my mind—I talk myself into disregarding them using fear as a motivation. That is not hypocritical. I am *trying* to believe and should eventually be rewarded for it."

"Good luck with your interpretation," I said "I hope your god sees your point and forgives you for the faux pas."

"Look here," he said getting on the offensive, trying to atone for his previous sin. "You keep criticizing all religions, but what have you got to offer in return? I have been hearing your condemnations of everything religious for over five years now, but I've never heard anything from you that's constructive—just unadulterated negativism. I won't listen to any more of your *holier than thou* arguments until you come up with a better philosophy of life than the ones you are criticizing. Give me something I can believe in that makes my life joyous and contented, without doubts and feelings of guilt, and I will be happy to follow you around."

"Forget it—I don't want anyone following me around," I replied.

But he was right, of course. And I quickly realized that criticizing religion was not enough. I had to come up with a convincing alternative or stop the criticisms—*put up or shut up* as the common cliché goes. What I came up with is all presented in the next chapter. It is more or less what I practice, so it was simply a question of organizing it and putting it down in writing.

I must remember to send a copy of the book to Abe, as soon as it comes out. Last time I saw him, he said he was still waiting. I didn't care for the look on his face when he said it.

2

NEO-HUMANISM:
A CREED FOR THE
NON-BELIEVER

The time has come to turn positive and start advancing a useful and practical philosophy of life without faith in a supreme being or membership in an organized religion. You will be in the minority if you adopt this type of life, often scorned and sometimes shunned from some groups and activities. In theocratic countries, you might be seriously persecuted, even prosecuted and imprisoned. You are most fortunate if you live in one of the multicultural societies of the western nations, especially in a big city, where there is more tolerance for unusual beliefs.

I will now be taking the positive side of the ensuing arguments. Advancing new positions is always tougher than arguing against existing ones—it is usually harder to build than to tear down.

I have named the proposed creed *Neo-humanism*. It is not a religion. It is just a set of reasonable answers to the complex questions of human existence. There is nothing divine or sacred about these answers.

Who Made This World And Why?

Most religions claim that a god created the universe and all life in it in so many days. The reason he created it, they go on to claim, is so that he can reign over it like a lord over his plebeian subjects. We, the pawns, are to devote our entire existence around this god—to be forever consumed by his presumed ubiquitous presence and perennial demands. We are directed to love him, worship him, fear him, obey *his* rules, and most importantly, to pay out part of our income to his local representatives on the planet. *God forbid* if there really was such a god, so egomaniacal and vain, that he had to create a whole world for the sole purpose of reigning over it. He now—presumably—sits around in some unspecified location, demanding that his subjects love and worship him, throwing thunderbolts of catastrophes at those who don't—sometimes even at those who do, just to keep them in line. Such a god would not be worth our attention, let alone our respect and devotion.

"Sorry, but I disagree, completely!"

It was my wife, Estelle, butting in and interrupting, just as I was gaining momentum with my aphorisms. She has a knack for doing that, an innate ability to bring on the chaos. Estelle had already raised serious objections to some of the argumentation of the first chapter. She plays an even greater role in the discussions that follow.

Estelle has been my wife for 40 plus years, and is a devout Christian. She has been tolerating my ravings for even longer, back from the time of our courting days. I often use her as a sounding board for the development of my theories—it's a way to uncover weak points, or tie up loose ends. Besides, she is the only one left to argue with. We do have 3 sons, but they are too busy to argue, and they are closer to me on this issue, anyway. As for all my religious friends, they all vanished long ago—looking for greener proselytizing pastures.

My arguments with Estelle provoke the mind to a sharper focus of the issues and lead to improved dissection of new ideas. Sometimes I even admit defeat—an intentional act of hypocritical magnanimity. I don't want her to become frustrated and quit on me—I need her to complete the manuscript. Stand-up comedians have been using their wives as imaginary sidekicks for decades. The time has come to use one as a devil's advocate in a serious endeavor—like this here book. Good luck!

"You disagree?" I asked her.

"Yes, I do. Of course, God expects us to love and worship Him—He created us, we are His children. You did exactly the same thing with your children, didn't you? I've seen your beaming face when they looked at you adoringly—don't you deny it. And, by the way, doesn't that prove that He created you, in His own image?"

Estelle always enunciates the word *god* with a special intonation that oozes respect, admiration and awe. Not unlike most priests, ministers, evangelists and the like.

"What it proves is that man made up a god in his image.

I wanted to stop the conversation at that point—I'd give her the last word if she'd let me think up an answer to the major question of the chapter. But she wouldn't

"I hear you mocking the Church's answer, but your first idea on creation is that man created God—prrrrrr," Estelle shouted, blowing air though her pursed lips to make a scoffing noise. "That hardly qualifies for an answer to the question. Do I sense here that you don't really have one?"

I have to admit here that Estelle was right; I don't have much to offer here, nothing different from what is already known—pretty much zilch, in my opinion. So, let me just critique some of the existing answers, and then tell you my opinion about the whole issue.

As we noted earlier, religions claim that some god did it, in so many days [55], though the duration of these days is vague, often stretched to millennia, depending on the incongruity of the religious argument on hand. Science claims that life started as an accident, and then it evolved, following rules that tend to improve the various forms of life—making them more adaptable to the ever-changing environment.

"There you go again, sneaking in a slanderous statement, that stuff about the duration of the days of creation," Estelle remarked as soon as she saw what I had written here. "Nothing vague about it, the good book says 6 days. Now, does anyone know the duration of days when the book was written? No! Nobody does. The good book is precise—people's knowledge is questionable. That's all."

I had to ignore her otherwise I would never complete this section.

Personally, I am unable to accept that some god did it. It is not really an answer—it's magic. Not only that! Religions have a pretty inadequate answer to the question of why *he did it*— his *motive* for the act. After all, in every good whodunit—and the creation of the world is the *ultimate* one—the perpetuator has a motive. The church's idea of an acceptable motive—we already noted—is that god created this world so that its creatures can chronically and habitually thank him. Gee, I don't know what kind of hallelujahs he expects from mosquitoes and snakes. Even if we accept that some god did it, I don't think his motive is known, nor do I think he wants me on my knees day and night thanking him.[9]

So, I say "NO" to this answer. It's not good enough.

Now let us look at science. The most widely accepted theory regarding the creation of the universe is the Big Bang theory[10] [50,52-54]. But it is not the only one, so we don't have anything that's considered the definitive answer on the subject. Then there is science's most commonly accepted theory of the creation of life [49,51], which contends that it happened in the water as the result of an accident. Oh, it's easy enough to accept that a bunch of chemical elements would combine together in an electrical storm to create an amino acid—protoplasm, whatever—in some distant swamp or sea. It might even happen again on some other planet. But to accept that from this start-up molecule, this miniscule amoeba, there was a glorious jump to whales, elephants, gorillas and humans—that sounds magical even to a devout scientist like myself. Lucky for science it doesn't need to come up with a motive—if the whodunit's

---

[9] Deism advocates that god created this universe and then lost interest is his creation [32-35].

[10] The Big Bang Theory was originally proposed by George Lemaξtre (a Belgian Priest) in 1927.

doer was an accident, no motive needs to be articulated. About the only thing that makes science's answer plausible is that it took *eons* to evolve from the amoeba to the present life forms, and many things can happen over eons. Even so, I say to science, *"you are not there yet, keep trying."*

So far then, we have a preposterous religious answer—barely palatable even to the faithful—and some plausible ones by science that need additional work.

Now here is my answer.

Who cares? Sure it would be nice to know who did it (that is the whole point of a good whodunit), but it would not probably change my life, unless the guy shows up, and demands compensation. This being highly unlikely, not knowing the answer is no different than watching a TV mystery with the screen going blank in the last five minutes. Or reading a mystery and discovering that the final pages are missing. It upsets you for a while, but you don't go out and devote your life to someone who claims to know the results.

When I visited the Grand Canyon in Arizona and Utah, I marveled at the thing for hours, the way I often marvel at the whole cosmos. Its magnitude and beauty demanded an explanation on how it came to be. Would you be happy with a "God made it"? As it was, the local information center was happy to oblige, and I had an earful. But to tell you the truth, I no longer remember this explanation, nor do I care that I don't. The key event is that I was delighted to have seen the magnificent canyon.

Likewise, the most important pursuit in life is not to seek the answer to the question of who made this world and why. It is to marvel at it—to be delighted to have had the good luck to visit it. It is to seek a meaningful and contented life while you are a part of it.

"Can I have one small digression here, before you continue on your profound diatribe?" Estelle asked when she saw me getting ready to close this section. "I just want to tell the reader, that it is just like you to start your philosophy of life without even a good answer to the first question. I hope they didn't fall for *the question is unimportant* routine.

"OK, I don't have an answer to the first question—I have already admitted it," I said. "But the cosmogony that you believe in is pure poppycock. I am writing a serious book here, and I am not about to lie to the reader. I am not going to give him fairy tales, when I haven't the foggiest of how this world came about."

"I take issue with your characterizations of our Creation Science," she replied resentfully.

"It is not a science," I replied. "The religious fanatics decided to call it a science so that they can include it in the public school curriculum. It was an ingenious artifice—I grant—because the Constitution prohibits the teaching of religious courses in public schools. You call this childish explanation of the origin of the universe a science—I call it a contempt for human intelligence."

"I disagree. It explains the creation, doesn't it? And nobody has been able to disprove it."

"It explains it with one phrase—*god did it*," I replied. "It is the same phrase that religions use to explain any phenomenon not yet fully understood by science. Is that your idea of a science? Apparently all that the students have to learn during the entire semester is the phrase, *god did it*, and they…ace the course. Good night!"

But she didn't hear what I said—she left the room before I started my last remarks. She does that a lot—she throws out a jab and then leaves the room, making sure she wins the point. But I don't mind—I don't have to win every exchange. I don't have a monkey on my back. I know who I am.

Why Are We Here?

Why are we here on this planet? Is there some *meaning* to our existence? Are we in some kind of *mission* as we pass through the short interlude of our life? If we are, can we lead happy and contented lives pursuing this mission? And how do we determine what is right and what is wrong—ethical or unethical—so that human relationships are peaceful and fair?

Religions claim to have the answers to all these questions. They postulate the existence of a deity and then the mantra becomes the same as in the previous section. We are here because this god created us. Our mission is to serve him, love him and fear him. Meaning in life is attained through belonging to this or that religion, accepting some prophet or son of god as our savior and obeying rigorously some dogmas, rules, rituals and the like. And if you reject these answers, you are headed directly to eternal damnation. That's not very nice.

Do I have some different answers to these questions? And do my answers form a solid foundation for the development of an acceptable philosophy of life without gods or religions?

That's the contention here—the major reason for writing this book. The answers that I will provide have served me as useful guidelines for sunrise-to-sunset joyous and satisfying living for more than five decades. I could become even happier, if a large section of the population bought this book—my standard of living will rise significantly. However, no further commitment is asked of the reader. Once the book is read, you are on your own to accept or reject its assertions. There will be no black-robed chaperones to ensure that you follow the path, no fiery preachers calling you serpents or generation of vipers if you stray from it. There will be no bloodcurdling threats of hellfire if you refuse to embrace its principles, and no demands for a cut of your hard-earned salary to maintain elaborate temples and opulently draped high priests. And I won't ask anyone to spend any of his precious time perpetually reading and re-interpreting this here book.

I believe that all such questions can be reduced to three major parts, and these parts dictated most of the organization of this chapter.

The first part deals with the question of why we have been placed on this earth—whether we are here to fulfill some specified mission. This part will be discussed in two sections. The present section will introduce this subject and propose a general mission without analyzing it in detail. The following section will be devoted to a detailed interpretation and analysis of this mission. These two sections form the foundation of a philosophy of life for the non-believer.

The second part deals with the issue of good vs. evil or right vs. wrong—the moral foundation of our existence. This will be taken up in the third section. Every philosophy of life must suggest ways to differentiate *good* from *evil—they serve as the foundation of social and personal morality.* Since non-believers are often accused of lacking a basis for making moral judgments, this section is quite vital to the development.

The last part deals with the question of happiness and contentment in a life without religion and it will be discussed in detail in the fourth section.

The final section of the chapter deals with the existence of the state, demonstrating that its major role is to aid the citizenry in the pursuit of their missions.

The entire theory is developed without any reference to god (or gods) or some man-created religion. It will gradually become apparent that such things are not needed for the formulation of the mission, that they are not needed for the development of a sound moral code and that they are certainly not needed for the attainment of happiness and fulfillment in life. They are not needed—period. In fact, they may even be a hindrance to the attainment of these goals.

So why are we here on this planet? What is our overall mission in life?

Well, the answer that I have adopted is based on the...*Christian bible* [55]. It is in Genesis, Chapter 1, verse 28. No, it's no hoax—nor a cruel joke. Besides, I am not going to adopt it literally—I plan to expand and modernize it considerably in the next section.

So what did god say to the people after he created them in his own image? He told them to go down to earth and to *"Be fruitful and multiply, and replenish the earth, and subdue it."*

I want the reader to note that according to the authoritative source of Christianity and Judaism, that's all he…spake. He didn't tell them to go down there and spend all their time *worshipping him* as most Christian denominations demand, or *loving his son, Jeeeesus,* as most Christian evangelists keep shouting. He didn't say that their mission was to stay on their knees praying to him for their salvation, nor to seek out his representatives on earth and submit to their dictates. And he didn't instruct humans to go down there and waste their time…reading the bible.

"What are you doing?" Estelle shrieked when she saw me referring to the bible. "What sort of trick is that, writing an anti-Christian book and quoting the Bible in support of your arguments? The Bible is a Sacred Book. You have no right to contaminate it by exploiting it, especially after bad-mouthing it all your life."

"I am not quoting the bible as a sacred book—as if it were god's word," I countered. "The bible is just a book—an interesting one, I concede. It is actually an anthology—a collection of works written by various authors. I have the right to quote it without accepting its contents as sacrosanct—authors can do that as long as they credit the original source properly. I am not quoting god himself—just the guy who wrote a specific passage. In this case, we don't even know who the bloke is—the statement is in the old testament. Don't you worry, though, you'll never see me walking around like a peacock, making a living by waving The Holy Book at people's faces. And incidentally, I am not writing an anti-Christian book, just a pro-non-Christian or rather a pro-non-religious book."

"In any event," I concluded before she had time to dissect my last sophism, "your objections are overruled! My intentions are to resurrect this Biblical answer—whether you like it or not. It is my firm conviction that the guy who wrote this passage in the Old Testament had it right."

"So that's going to be your answer? That we are here just to procreate?" Estelle barked, bursting out into uncontrollable laughter. "You didn't need the Bible for that! Countless people have suggested it before. Godless scientists enamored with Darwin's theory of evolution, communists bent on destroying the spirituality of humankind, religious *contrarians* or atheists, confused agnostics, the list can go on and on. And they were all chased out of town. I sure hope that you have something new to add. I don't feel like…moving again."

I ignored Estelle and continued on with my interpretation of the bible's passage.

God's first words were to *be fruitful.* I take fruitful to mean fertile, so this utterance was not a directive—it was intended as a divine bestowment of the ability to reproduce. This ability was needed to fulfill the ensuing directive of their mission—*to multiply and replenish the earth.* I want everyone to note now that to multiply and restock the earth with new generations of humans was the major task of their assigned mission. I am ranking it the number one task in my proposed mission as well. Not because god said it—there is no need for such a belief—but because I find that it forms a solid foundation for a human mission that leads to a meaningful, fruitful and contented life.

"To subdue the earth," was a way of saying to be successful in your fight for survival. When the phrase was written, humans lived in agrarian societies. The fight for food and water was harsh—the environment was cruel and unforgiving. Subduing the earth would guarantee survival—even prospering. That's why it was added to the human mission.

God's directive was straightforward and to the point. Go down to earth, multiply and prosper—ensuring the replenishing of the human species. That was the mission.

So why was this simple but powerful human assignment totally ignored by the Christian and Jewish religions? Why was it replaced by the notion that our primary task is to love and worship the creator?

It is my opinion that this occurred for two principal reasons.

The first reason was that placing god at the center of the human existence places the church there as well, handing them the power and influence always sought by human institutions. There is no reason to expand on this—Estelle would have a field day with her protestations of outrage.

The second one is that the words were given such an exegesis that the church decided to *de-emphasize and distance itself* from them. The dictated duty "to multiply" was taken to mean "to procreate"—to copulate and produce offspring. This put a high priority on having sex, and the clergy didn't want people to enjoy sex—not as long as *they* had to abstain from it. It was swiftly decided that mere multiplication and preservation of the species was a mission worthy only of animals—that humans were destined for loftier, more spiritual goals in their existence.

And it wasn't only the church. The idea had been rejected in the past even in non-religious circles. Intellectuals of all types (philosophers, scientists, literary figures, etc) attacked it with vengeance. The notion that humans were the highest order on this planet was ever pervasive. It provided everyone with a feeling of superiority and arrogance. Humans had intellect, ability to manipulate the environment and awareness of self—all these presumably absent in all other forms of life. Anyone suggesting similarities in the mission of humans and animals is intellectually and spiritually suspect—even immoral and evil.

So Estelle was right about this issue. With such a history behind it, reviving the original biblical mission will be a serious challenge. I better have something more to contribute, something that raises the mission from an erroneously perceived procreating activity to a more noble and spiritually uplifting endeavor. And I do—I plan to develop the expanded mission in detail in the next section. I am just laying the foundation for this larger task here.

Let me start by noting that over the last century or so, we have started to realize that all life forms a gigantic ecosystem. Safeguarding the survival of a species is not only important for each plant or animal, but also necessary for the survival of all life on our planet. In fact, the whole of the ecosystem is so intertwined, that the disappearance of one species could create a chain reaction—a holocaust.

By and by, avoiding extinction even of the lowliest life form starts to become important—to gain respect and *nobleness*. Organizations are created that keep track of an animal or plant species and how it is perpetuating itself. Actions that could undermine the survival of a species are condemned. Governments pass environmental laws, many dealing with the protection of endangered species. The hunting of such animals or the harvesting of such plants becomes an anathema—universally forbidden. The capture and swift punishment of violators becomes an example for emulation.

All these developments lead to a new conscience of existence, a new reverence for all life—unprecedented in the chronicles of mankind. It is gradually realized that humans are not here to rape the environment—to subjugate it to human desires—but rather to serve as its guardian and protector. Young people take passionately to the new task—the protection of this or that species threatened by extinction. If saving any species is noble and worthy of a person's lifework, why is personally contributing to the well being of the human species unworthy of a mission in life?

"Whatever happened to Spencer?" I asked Estelle without raising my eyes from the manuscript, pretending to be making idle conversation. I knew what had happened to him, but I threw out the question as bait.

"You mean Spencer Mayberry, the young zoologist, the son of the Lutheran Minister in Minneapolis?" she replied. "I thought you had totally forgotten him. The whole family left Minneapolis and went to live in Africa for a spell—missionary work, if I am not mistaken. Not the kind of thing you'd acknowledge as significant work, I am sure."

"No, I recall Spencer well," I replied, happy that she had taken the bait. "Wasn't he the one who organized a demonstration to stop the residential zoning of a Minneapolis suburb because it threatened the survival of some sort of horny toad?" I asked, shuffling some manuscript pages, pretending to have only a mild interest in the issue.

"Yes, he is the one, though the protest might have been for some bat," Estelle replied. "Well, the latest is that he has decided to devote his entire life to save a rare rodent from extinction in some remote desolate tract in Africa. I am really proud of our new generation of young people, aren't you? Chasing the buck is no longer top priority in their life—they view doing good for the world as much more meaningful. I always knew that Spencer had godliness in him—that he would devote his life to something worthy and noble. Of course, being the son of a Minister had a lot to do with it, *but you will never admit it.*"

"Oh, maybe it did!" I replied. "I didn't realize that you admired individuals who devote their entire lives to saving obscure animals from extinction."

"Of course I do," she replied. "I am just as concerned about our environment as the next person, and saving a species from extinction is job one, isn't it?"

"Yes, it certainly is," I replied. I was up out of my chair now, pacing the floor, ready to pounce. She had dug a perfect hole for herself.

"Perhaps you can explain to me then, why saving a rat is a worthy mission in life, but pursuing the same goal for the human species is not!"

Her face turned red. She looked dazed, speechless, gasping for air. I knew that it was time for the coup de grace—before she had time to recover.

"So now you agree that my answer for our basic mission in life is correct?" I asked, with phony astonishment on my face. "Do I also sense that you are starting to suggest that the church should be given credit for this notion? Was that why you tried to correlate Spencer's decision with his religious upbringing?"

I will not relate Estelle's answer to the reader—I am sure she regrets it already. She has apologized for it, anyway. All I was trying to do was to get her to admit that the notion that we are here on this earth to "be fruitful and multiply" is a respectable basic goal for our existence. It is not the entire mission, but it is a fundamental and crucial part.

She had unwittingly done so, of course, but she demanded—and I agreed later—that it was because of...*entrapment.* I've got to keep her happy—till this book project is over, anyway.

How Do We Fulfill Our Mission?

"So you are about to expound on the basic mission?" Estelle asked one evening after I wrote down the above title. "What else is there besides procreation?"

"There is a whole host of things, including even the writing of a book like this one," I replied.

"Really?" she exclaimed—her eyes nearly out of their sockets with astonishment. "Isn't that nice and convenient! First you write a book about a new godless philosophy of life. Then you declare that the writing of such a book is part of a new mission in life. All that's left for you is to declare yourself the Lord of this new sect and climb on a throne." She added with a cackle.

"Calm down," I replied, "you won't see me emulating your usual religious founders—declaring my book sacred and making a bonfire of the rest. I am only proposing a new philosophy of life here—not a new religion."

"But you just said that this book is a contribution to the mission," she countered angrily.

"You will soon see why writing this book—any book, really—is part of the mission, but not till I am good and ready. Do you want to hear it or not?"

"I am all ears," she said sarcastically—her anger somewhat defused.

"OK, here's what I have in mind. It is one thing to propose a general mission, and quite another thing to list the various activities that *promote it*. We have already noted that one of the reasons that the clergy opposed it was because they interpreted it too narrowly. They assumed that it could be accomplished by one thing and one thing alone—sex."

"But isn't sex the only effective way to multiply?"

"Yes, though not always to thrive and prosper," I replied. "Reproduction is the paramount way of contributing to the mission, of course. Some tribes have, in fact, considered it so important that they reverted to some rather intriguing ways to encourage it. In one African culture, a man is not considered a man unless he produced an offspring. People ignore him, his opinion is ridiculed, and he has no vote in local affairs, until he contributes to the tribe by having a child. At that very instant he assumes his identity *as the father of the newborn child* and is embraced by all. In this culture the act of contributing a new person is the principal act of a person's life—the act that finally *certifies* him as an *acceptable* member of the society."

"Isn't that extreme?"

"Yes, it is, and I am not advocating it here." I continued. "I just brought it up to show that there is at least one culture where the zenith of one's life is producing an offspring. In such a culture, the reward for having a child is very high. But so is the punishment of failing to have one—a lifetime of shunning, isolation and despair. Even in western cultures there is some stigma associated with non-mating and non-procreation. Women are often the prime victims—humiliated with derogatory labels like spinster, old-maid and the like."

"But producing the maximum number of children is not enough for a nation to proliferate and evolve," I continued. "It is, as the mathematicians say, *necessary but not sufficient.* The nation can be overwhelmed with overpopulation and lose its way—self-destruct."

"All right, then. Isn't it about time to start naming some other activities that promote your mission of survival?" Estelle shouted. "The suspense is killing me here."

"OK. I'll start right now. To begin with, everyone has an obligation to survive, otherwise the total number of people is reduced and the species suffers. Giving up on life is not an option—dead people make no contributions."

"That makes sense," Estelle remarked. "Religions do not condone suicide, either—it is a sin."

"Yes, sure, they call it a sin. But when people face real difficulties in their fight for survival, they confuse them with fatalistic phrases such as *god will provide* or *put your faith in god,* and the like. Here we are emphasizing that individual survival is up to each one of us and that it is a deep and profound obligation to the species. Religions are too pre-occupied with god and their own power to be forceful on this issue. Their obsession with their artificial concepts of god's love and power, heaven, allegiance to the church, etc. lead to ambivalence and pusillanimity of conviction. Having abandoned the original biblical mission hasn't helped matters either."

"OK, OK, you made your point. What is next in the details of your mission?"

"Well, I think one must do his best to realize his maximum potential—to rise as high as he can in the hierarchical structure of his society."

"Are you suggesting that getting into the rat race of social climbing is part of our mission in life? Isn't this unbecoming of a freethinker of your stature? You are starting to sound like a two-bit motivational speaker now. How does that square off with your overall mission of survival? Can't you simply survive without stepping on others to get ahead?"

"Achieving one's maximum potential is a duty of immense weight to the mission. A high rank in the society begets a high standard of living and consequently it leads to a wider and better choice of mates. This, in turn, increases the chances that the children are a worthily improved replenishment of the species. It also aids in the fulfillment of the rest of one's mission much more successfully. You can give this part of the mission a bad spin if you like, but its importance is quite obvious to students of human evolution. Of course, seeking one's maximum potential causes conflicts with others who are also doing the same. That's where morality and the law come in to ensure that the maneuvering is fair and that the rules of the game are respected and understood by all."

Estelle turned thoughtful and reflective. It was her way of acknowledging that the point was sound.

"Do you have some advice on how to reach one's maximum potential?"

"The best advice is to understand your strengths and weaknesses and pursue a course based on your strengths. The worst advice is to trust in god or in his earthly stand-ins. But I don't want to oversimplify this issue. It is one of the hardest things for people to do—humans have difficulty understanding themselves and their potential. Doing this issue justice would require a whole new book.

There are hundreds of them out there—it is a favorite subject among motivational writers, inspirational gurus and the like. So I am going to continue with my topic here—elaborating on activities that promote the mission."

"Fine."

"With one's personal survival assured and his pursuit of his goals on track," I went on, "he must turn his attention to activities that lead to the ultimate act of the mission—reproduction. He must seek a suitable mate, fall in love, marry and have children—as many children as he can successfully handle—and refocus his efforts for continual survival to his family unit. He must properly parent the children so that they, in turn, can follow the same cycle. He must also help his children raise their offspring. These, and many others, are acts that he must pursue to help himself and his family survive and prosper, which in turn contribute to the thriving of his society. In short, he can't walk around impregnating women at random, producing stray children with no chance of flourishing and then claim that he is aiding the species to multiply. That would be counterproductive to the mission that is espoused in the book. It will also turn out to be immoral as we will see in due time—in the section on ethics."

"I see," Estelle replied. "I have to admit that you have adorned the fundamental mission with a lot of auxiliary activities to make it more palatable. That's very clever, indeed."

"It wasn't done intentionally. It is pretty obvious that all these activities are vital to the mission—that mere procreation does not guarantee a successful replenishment of the species."

"What about acts in defense of country and society? They promote survival of the species so they are part of the mission, right?"

"The answer is a categorical yes. You are referring, of course, to heroic acts in the battlefield or during calamitous events like fires, earthquakes, hurricanes, tornadoes and the like. Protecting the whole is just as important as contributing members to it. Many societies already recognize, appreciate and reward such acts, turning them into examples for emulation. A nation's history consists mostly of descriptions of the lives of its heroes and their valiant, larger-than-life acts."

"Just one minute here," Estelle interrupted. "If defending your territory and culture is a major contribution to the mission, then defending one's religion—part of the culture—should also be part of his mission, right?"

"No," I replied.

"Why not?" she asked resentfully.

"Because I am developing a non-believer's mission in life. Non-believers have no religion so your argument is moot. You can bring this issue up in the next meeting of your church elders—they might incorporate it in their mission."

She was thrown off a bit but she recovered rapidly.

"Yeah, OK, but this whole new interpretation of the mission still lacks humanity—something that would appeal to the intellect, the spirituality, the soul. After all, most of the acts you listed so far are also performed by animals, and...."

"I have some of that too!" I interrupted.

"You do?" Estelle inquired with disbelief.

"You bet! There are two new things that I am throwing into the mission. The first one concerns our environment—our planet."

"Our environment? You are not going to exploit the environment to sell this opprobrious book, are you?" Estelle asked petulantly. "Would you stoop that low for the sake of popularity?"

"I am not seeking popularity, for I don't need any. I am not reaching out for converts—I made that clear in the prologue. The concern for the environment is part of our mission because all life is intertwined. We are all part of the same ecosystem and ignoring one species may lead to another's extinction. This, in turn, may start a domino effect that culminates into a cataclysmic event that sweeps our own species away. So brutal self-centrism does not promote the mission. Respect for all life on this planet is essential for the continuing successful evolution of humanity. It is our duty to continue to study all life and its interrelationships. It is essential that we gain further understanding of the interplay of life so that we don't make some fatal mistake for the sake of a goal that serves human survival in the short term. Helping other species in their pursuit of survival may have been considered a lofty endeavor

91

among naturalists and boy scouts in the past. But it is time we all understood that it serves our own self-interest—our own better survival. That's how it becomes part—an indispensable part—of our own mission," I concluded forcefully.

Estelle stared out toward the lake in silent agreement. Religions had started to come around in adopting such causes in recent years. Their justification had god in it—it always does. They always assume that their followers are incapable of rational thinking.

Just then Estelle left and returned some time later with a freshly brewed pot of coffee. I could smell it as she approached the den where these exchanges were consummated.

"The second one is culture," I said after she filled the cups.

"Culture?"

"You betcha," I replied triumphantly. "A society needs to develop and continuously grow a strong and vibrant culture. Without it, it will perish. People die to preserve their culture—they are quick to make accusations of cultural genocide if their culture is being undermined. There is no doubt that culture *is a necessary* element for the blossoming of a tribe, and thus any contribution to culture is an integral part of the mission."

She tried to interrupt me, but I wouldn't let her—not while I was on this high horse.

"Now, do you see how the writing of a book is part of the mission? It adds to the culture—that's how. So are painting, sculpturing, creating music, dancing and acting on the stage or in movies—any cultural contribution. In times of war, these activities are not a major part of the mission—they are in a lower tier of importance. In times of peace, their significance skyrockets."

I raised my voice a bit when I mentioned painting, in order to give it enough emphasis for her to notice. Estelle dabbled in oils—she fancied herself a pretty fair amateur artist.

She realized it and a hint of a smile surfaced on her face. I also sensed that she was beginning to realize that I had a sound argument. Even so, she wasn't about to give up the fight—packing it in early wasn't part of her temperament. My flattery appeared to have only a slight effect on her.

"What about believing in God and participating in religious

activities?" she snapped. "Isn't that also part of the culture? Isn't that what you claimed in your other book [1] and what we agreed in one of your dialogues in the first chapter?"[11]

"Religion is part of the culture," I replied. "But believing in some god or participating in some religious activity is not going to be included in the mission here."

"Isn't that inconsistent and unfair? People sacrifice even their lives for their right to practice their religion, and you are excluding it?"

"I am not even considering it. I am writing a book whose main point is that religion is redundant. But even if I considered it, I would exclude it. Engaging in religious activities is like taking part in the activities of a political party, watching a movie or a football game, or being part of the festivities on Independence Day. You are a fan of culture and not a creator of it. Now, if you write a treatise on *religious ethics and its effects on today's teenagers* or a basketball playbook, those would be considered a part of the mission. Passive participation in an activity and blind devotion to some specific ideology are not part of the mission—of a non-believer, anyway. For believers, on the other hand—it may be the entire mission," I added smiling.

Estelle was too absorbed in her thoughts to notice my last jab.

"You know," she said after a long pause, "I think it is time for you to summarize all these activities that promote your mission. Not a long diatribe now, just a short, snappy statement."

"Good idea," I replied. "Let me do so in the style of a scientific presentation. First, I will present a general mission statement, and then I will outline the specific activities that buttress it. They are organized into two groups—activities that contribute directly to the mission and those that do so indirectly. Close scrutiny of the entire list indicates that the emphasis is on the promotion and celebration of life in all of its forms and manifestations."

---

[11] The one entitled, "And Man Created God."

GENERAL STATEMENT

Our mission in life is to give our best effort for the perpetuation and successful evolution of our species.

Primary Contributions: (First Tier)
A. *To individually survive in the face of all adversity.*
B. *To realize our maximum individual potential.*
C. *To go through the cycle of mating, producing offspring, parenting and grand-parenting.*
D. *To defend our territory and culture in the face of internal or external threats.*
E. *To engage in acts which promote the environment and the preservation and successful evolution of all life on the planet.*

Secondary Contributions: (Second Tier)
A. *To contribute to the culture of the society.*
B. *To engage in philanthropic and altruistic acts toward the more needy members of society.*
C. *To contribute to fields that improve life such as medical professions, teaching professions, engineering, food growing, etc.*

"By the way," I said after I finished the list, "the world is presently divided into separate nations, so everyone's point of reference is his own country—his own society. When we refer to activities that enable the human species to propagate and prosper, we are talking about the part of the species that lives in our own country. It is hoped that sometime in the future, we will be able to pursue the mission with reference to the entire humankind. In the meantime, countries concentrate mainly on their own survival, occasionally clashing with each other, as we will eventually see in the sequel."

"That is much clearer, thank you." Estelle nodded with approval. "The list follows the order of our previous discussion. About the only thing that we did not discuss are the last two items on the second tier of the list."

"Let's discuss them now then," I replied.

"Fine, let's start with the second item," Estelle suggested, "philanthropic acts in the aid of the less fortunate members of the society. The church has always encouraged such acts—Christianity is almost synonymous with them. I see that you are including them as part of your mission as well. Did you borrow this idea from the Old Testament where Good Samaritanism originated?"

"I didn't need to," I replied. "Philanthropy is broadly the act of helping others to achieve their missions. Helping the needy is obviously important to the mission—if they are not helped they may perish and the species will decrease in numbers. It is especially crucial to help orphaned children because children represent the future of the society—the next replenishment of the species. Religions do advocate such activities, but they have never explained why—they have never tied them to some general principle generic to their dogma. I must admit though that promoting philanthropy has served them well. The faithful are convinced that you have to be a believer to be a Good Samaritan, which is an unfortunate misunderstanding of the need for the concept."

Estelle looked at me peevishly but did not utter any objections.

"By the way," I went on, "there is also a misunderstanding of the type of aid that the less fortunate people need. Food, toys, medicine, etc. are all fine because they help with their basic survival, but they are not a solution to their long-term problems—they treat the symptoms rather than the disease. Of equal and possibly of greater importance is help in attaining their optimum potential—an important item in fulfilling their mission. For then, they can break the bondage of philanthropic dependence—in many cases governmental welfare—and pursue the rest of their mission on their own. But that will not come easily without a well-articulated and universally accepted mission in life, because at present the center of everyone's preoccupation is god and the institutions of faith."

Estelle appeared to have tired of the issue and started to stare at the list.

"The last item on the list is also interesting and, I guess, self-explanatory," she remarked.

"Yes, but not all inclusive. Any profession that helps people with their mission or promotes life at large can be included in this item. And all such professions are highly respected by the populace."

"Yes, I have noticed that, but why? Why is teaching, for example, considered a noble profession even though teachers are underpaid? Why is a high school teacher often more revered than the local liquor store owner or the section manager of a department store? They may both have the same amount of education."

"Well, I think it's because people instinctively realize that teachers (and medical doctors) are fulfilling two of their mission goals at the same time. They have succeeded in reaching a high level of personal potential, and they are helping others to reach theirs in the daily exercise of their profession."

"Gee, you are right. I guess they are involved in a mission activity while working. I can see where that would be quite satisfying—if I agreed with any of this, which I don't," she hastened to add.

"Do you have any other comments about the list or the general mission?" I asked smiling.

"Yes, I do. Looking over this entire list I see that most of the activities in the third item of the first tier—marriage, bearing children, raising the children, grand-parenting, etc.—have been the cornerstones of most religions. In fact, some religions have elevated some of these—weddings, baptisms, etc—to holy sacraments."

"You are correct in saying that religions strongly encourage many of these as part of their repertory of blessed activities. But since people are naturally drawn to most of these, all they do is belabor the obvious. As for elevating them to the level of sacraments—an artificial status—that was done for additional fanfare, pomposity and self-importance. And it worked. It has gained them an air of indispensability—the illusion that the church is necessary to *render these activities valid.* It is quite subtle and frightfully clever—no question about that."

"You are attributing evil motives to religions without proof."

"You are right—I am sorry. So, let's think of it in a reverse manner. Why do you *need* the church to control or approve these activities? Which one can you NOT perform without its help, or authorization? Is it falling in love? Going a-courting? Getting married? Performing in bed? Parenting or grand parenting?"

96

"Well, OK, maybe you don't need the church, but it is a nice warm feeling to get their consent," she replied. "But you don't know anything about that—their blessing is an anathema to you."

"Look, I am not going to get into any personal polemics just now. I've got one rather important thing to say before I conclude this section—something rather unexpected and most likely controversial."

"Really? I thought the entire book could be described in such terms. Well, what is it?"

"It is that part of our mission—an important part—is...*death*," I shouted with an epideictic tone in my voice, emphasizing the last word to create the intended shock effect.

"Really? How does death fit in with your overall mission of perpetuating the species? If we all died, there would be no species. Are you not contradicting yourself here?"

"Death is part of the evolutionary cycle—not just for humans but for all living things. It is a major reason why humankind continues to flourish. If we all lived forever, the majority of the population would be old and decaying. The average well being of humanity would gradually decline and the successful evolution of the species would be jeopardized. Whoever espouses the proposed philosophy of life will understand this and will be able to face death fearlessly and without resentment—as an integral part of his mission in life."

"Then we ought to all commit suicide to speed up this process," Estelle snapped huffily.

"Very cute, but quite inaccurate. We have already condemned suicide as an act most foul—incongruous to the mission. I am talking about death from natural causes, usually occurring after one has fulfilled his mission to the best of his capability."

"Why didn't you include death in the list of your mission activities then?" Estelle asked. "Are you ashamed of it?"

I had to laugh. She has become a real stand-up comedian.

"No! It was a purposeful omission. Death, at present, is a mandatory part of our mission. And we all do it well—no one has found a way to fail in this contribution to the species."

Estelle was looking at me pensively trying to absorb the notion that death was part of our purpose in life.

"You see," I continued, "the creed I am proposing here has a sensible and logical explanation for death. No gods and no images of heaven or hell are needed. Non-believers feel that such concepts are naïve and insulting to their intelligence."

Estelle kept silent for a long time. I think I heard her muttering that she'd rather stay with her familiar images of heaven and hell, but I am not totally sure.

"What about people's perennial search for the fountain of youth? Why are they searching for eternal life if death is part of their mission?"

"These must be religious people trying to avoid paradise," I said smiling. "But they are not really searching for eternal life, they are searching for *eternal youth.* They wish to be forever young so that they can continuously go through the procreation cycle—the most important aspect of the mission."

"What if such a fountain of youth were found? Would death cease to be a part of your mission?"

"If people were able to live forever in a manner that the general mission is not compromised, then death would become a non-issue. Free thinkers are not frozen into some dogmatic position. As changes occur in the cosmos—naturally or by scientific advancement—all their positions can be re-evaluated vis-à-vis the general mission and can be changed."

"But you are frozen on the general mission you have proposed even though you are a free-thinker, right?" she asked coyly, realizing that she might have hit upon a contradiction.

"Well, yes. Because if that is undermined, there will be nobody around to debate the pros and cons of a new general mission," I answered laughing.

Estelle left the room for a bathroom break and returned looking refreshed.

"Have you got a name for your new philosophy of life?" She asked, realizing that it was time to change the subject.

"Do I need one?" I asked casually, pretending not to have thought much about the issue.

"I think so. It might help sell more books. A catchy name is an advantage when you propose something new—assuming it's new."

"I thought you wanted me to quit writing it. Now you are hoping for high sales?"

"Oh, I am thinking that if this breed of non-believers exists and is as numerous as you claim, what do I care if they buy this book? According to your admission, the book will not change anyone else's mind. Those who buy it already agree with you—they are lost souls, anyway. So let the cash registers ring—they benefit me as well, and I don't have to compromise my principles."

"I hear you," I replied glancing at her sideways. "Well, how about the name New Humanitarianism?"

"Is there some Old Humanitarianism philosophy of life?"

"No. But there is a *plain* Humanitarianism."

"What does this plain one advocate?"

I got up, picked up a dictionary, found the term and started reading.

"A Humanitarian is defined as a person who is broadly philanthropic and humane, one who believes that human nature is self-perfectible, one who holds that man's duty is limited to right-doing toward others and has an interest in the public welfare."

"Being philanthropic and humane, right-doing for others and having an interest in the public welfare are all quite noble and certainly part of the mission, but not the primary ways to contribute to the survival and vitality of humankind. Mating, producing and raising children—those are the major ways."

"And you don't feel that human nature is self-perfectible."

"No, I don't, but that's another issue. Returning to the name, I want to use the word Humanitarianism to stress that our primary duty is to the whole of *humanity*—and by induction to all forms of life. Yes, that may be it—the New Humanitarianism. Do you like it?"

"The problem I see with this name is the word *New*," Estelle persisted. "Centuries from now, it will still be the same theory, but it will no longer be *new*. And you won't be around to start calling it the Old Humanitarianism. You always scoff at cities named Newtown, criticizing the dead city fathers for their lack of foresight. Aren't you now falling into the same trap?"

"You have a point there," I replied. "OK, I'll name it Neo-humanitarianism then. It means the same thing, but putting the prefix neo, rather than the separate word *New*, eases the problem. They mean the same thing anyway."

"Now it is too long—nobody will be able to pronounce it, let alone remember it."

"All right then, I will make it shorter. I am naming it Neo-humanism."

"But does Humanism and Humanitarianism mean the same thing?"

"Not entirely. Philosophical Humanism is often thought of as F. C. S. Schiller's pragmatism [16-17], which emphasizes the idea that individual thought is the basis for personal truth. Humanists are quite active [18]. There are humanist groups and organizations all over the world. But we don't want to get too technical here. My Neo-humanism is not an effort to revive or strengthen the existing school. It is a new type of humanism."

"Neo-humanism? I still find it somewhat pretentious—even ostentatious. You might as well name it Nico-humanism. Better yet, why don't you concentrate on the major aspect of your new mission and call it *Procreationism?* Fornicate and prosper could be your new motto."

"Not bad," I replied laughing. "It might attract some of your comrades who espouse that oxymoronic science of *creationism*. They'll probably misinterpret the prefix and join in," I added, indicating no interest in continuing the dialogue.

I knew that Estelle's last sarcasm was also her last attempt to save some face. I could give her that—no problem. I am quite magnanimous.

Can Non-believers Have Morals?

The Moral Maxim

"What about questions of ethics?" Estelle remarked one afternoon as we were leaving for a walk around Lake Eola in downtown Orlando. "I seem to recall, from a basic course in Philosophy I took in college, that every philosophy of life should have a set of moral principles—a way to define good and evil. You did touch on the issue in one of your short dialogues in the previous chapter, but only to bash the ideas of the church. I don't recall that you proposed any constructive ideas of your own at the time, did you?"

"Well, no, I hadn't started to develop the theory just then," I replied. "Now would be the time to do it—I am glad you brought it up."

"You are planning a chapter on ethics, then?"

"No question about it. Judgments on human behavior are major aspects of our daily lives. Morality sets the rules of proper interaction between people while they are all engrossed in the pursuit of their missions. It also provides the guidelines for resolving conflicts and forms the foundation for the human legal system. By the way, one of the most common charges laid against non-believers is that they are immoral, or that their morality is personal and thus arbitrary. The faithful who make these charges believe, of course, that their morality comes directly from god. I aim to show that they are quite wrong in the sequel."

"Really? Can you give me the gist of it while we are riding in the car, or is it too complicated?"

"On the contrary," I replied. "I have a simple moral maxim—I can do it in a couple of short sentences. Here it goes.

"In the realm of Neo-humanism, good is anything that contributes to the successful execution of the proposed human mission. Bad is whatever hinders or endangers it. And if something does neither, it is morally neutral."

"That's it?"

"You bet. I can even make it shorter—in the form of a

101

commandment if you prefer. *Thou shall not put the hurt on the human mission.* It includes your ten commandments by the way—no need for Moses, plates, bush fires, nothing."

"It does?"

"Well, the ones that pertain to allowed (good) or prohibited (evil) *activities.* It does not cover the commandments that deal with god's bragging about being the only master of the universe, or about taking his name in vain and all that. Such things are irrelevant to the mission and according to the proposed maxim morally inconsequential."

"You feel that way because you don't believe in God, right?"

"Yes, and because I don't need—as religions do—to create a scary imaginary authority figure that sits on a throne and makes moral proclamations. Nor do I need to make up some silly story that creates the illusion that the commandments came directly from this authority. I have convincing arguments about the ethical nature of these acts. I can explain why they are good or bad, by relating them to our mission. I don't put out edicts that people should do this or that because *I am the man and I say so!*"

"You can quit your sarcasm and stick to the point, if you don't mind. Isn't your tying of good and evil to the mission an oversimplification of a rather complex issue?"

I took a little time to answer—I had to parallel park the car and needed to concentrate. We were soon walking around the lake, so I returned to our subject on hand.

Matters Of Life And Death

"Oversimplification, did you call it? Not really," I said. "Don't forget, I am giving you a general maxim here—a rational guiding moral principle for judging human behavior. It turns out that this principle does not alter the universally accepted view of most basic acts like killing, stealing, fornicating, etc. But it does more than that."

"What more does it do?"

"It serves as a guide in judging acts that are in the gray area—the moral dilemmas. Most religions do not have such a general guiding principle. When they announce that the act of killing or stealing are immoral, they mean killing or stealing *without a reason*. When moral controversies arise, they expect their…pontiff to resolve them. He usually does it in an arbitrary manner and the faithful sometimes become confused."

"What sort of moral controversies?"

"Moral dilemmas that are not resolvable by the absolute nature of the commandments. Killing to save your family from a murderous intruder, for example."

"Can you elaborate with some illustrations?"

"I will be delighted. Let's start with a simple case, the obviously disagreeable act of killing a human being. In Judaism and Christianity you have one of the ten commandments, *thou shall not kill*, which proclaims it to be an immoral act, a sin—whatever. However, the commandment does not give you a rational explanation why it should be so. *It is so because god proclaimed it to be so.*"

"The moral principle is the sanctity of life."

"Is it? I don't recall it being given as the reason for the commandment. But let us accept it for the time being. So if you are a Christian, you know that killing is immoral—it is forbidden by the commandment because of the sanctity of life. Now, suppose that an intruder attacks your family, and you kill him. Is that allowed? Is it moral?"

"Yes!" Estelle replied without any hesitation.

"On what basis?"

"Self defense, I think!"

"Oh, really. What happened to the sanctity of life? Did the commandment have a disclaimer clause in fine print, allowing killing under certain conditions?"

"I didn't say it did. But everyone knows that in self defense…."

"Self-defense is a legal concept—we are talking morality here. Didn't Jesus Christ preach that in such cases you must *turn the other cheek*? This was unprecedented, and he got plenty of good press for it—and he is still getting it. Yet everyone ignores it, as you just did. Moral confusion in abundance."

Estelle looked thoughtful for a few seconds.

"Now you see what I meant by moral dilemmas—they are an

everyday occurrence. What about wartime killing? Obviously, religions condone it and even encourage it. Why? Doesn't it conflict with the commandment?"

"I don't know. I never thought much about it—I assumed it was OK to kill the enemy during a war—I thought that the church had officially approved it. Maybe they consider it self-defense also."

"Self-defense for both countries at war? I am afraid you have to admit that there is a moral vacuum in your religion. A lot of impressive blah, blah, but when the dilemmas appear—moral uncertainty and equivocation. Most people assume that mere membership in a religion guarantees them a moral code and they feel superior to non-believers. But all it guarantees is that they have given up their right to judge morality to someone who claims to be god's spokesperson on the planet. Unfortunately—as I have just demonstrated—the moral code he dishes out is often flawed. The apotheosis of Christian confusion occurs in the case of...vendettas."

"Vendettas? How so?"

"Well, if you are a Christian, you've got two opposing views on vendettas. One comes from the old testament and says *an eye for an eye,* which is interpreted as *a life for a life.* The other comes from the new testament and is the ubiquitous *turn the other cheek* principle. Add now to the above the commandment on killing and you end up with a moral smorgasbord. That's what I meant by moral confusion—*chaos* is a better description—from the lack of a general moral principle."

"And how does your general moral principle solve such dilemmas?"

"I was hoping you'd ask," I replied smiling. "First, the act of killing without a reason is the epitome of evil—the antithesis of mission promotion. When you kill a person, you don't just endanger this person's pursuit of the mission; you stop him (or her) *dead* in his tracks—if you would permit me a word pun here. This is another reason why killing a child is so abhorrent—the child doesn't even get a chance to start on the pursuit of his own mission."

"That's interesting. I never thought of the murder of a child in this context."

"In addition, it doesn't take a genius to see that killing is an affront to the overall mission—murdering people in your own society can not help much in its perpetuation now, can it?"

"I guess not. Every time you kill, you reduce the number of living," Estelle added.

"Precisely. Now let's consider killing the intruder who threatened your family. The act of killing him is moral under the circumstances, because it aids the overall mission."

"How does it aid it?"

"Simple arithmetic. Isn't it better for the collective mission that one is killed, rather than an entire family? Besides, a primary part of an individual's mission is to stay alive and protect his family. Notice also that the maxim provides a moral justification for the principle of self-defense, which seems to be confusing to Christians vis-à-vis the *turn the other cheek* advice."

"Interesting."

"Now, let's move to the case of killing the enemy in a war situation. It, too, serves the mission. It aids in the survival of one's country and thus it is judged as honorable and good—even praiseworthy—on both sides of the conflict. Don't forget that we have referenced the mission to one's own country here and not the entire humankind. This causes a paradoxically moral dilemma in this case—both countries cannot be moral in killing each other's people—which we will take up again in the section on government."

"Interesting again."

"I hope you see that we can not judge killing as an act in itself—as the commandment does—and proclaim it unethical. You run into great moral difficulties that way. You must judge the act of killing in the context that it occurs and decide what it does to the mission in the overall balance."

"What about the vendetta issue?"

"It is ridiculously simple. A vendetta—revenge in general—has the effect of reducing the population and not allowing innocent people to pursue their own mission. It is the murder of an innocent person, which provokes the murders of other innocents. Bad all around—evil, immoral. You don't need to perform moral acrobatics through a set of conflicting pronouncements to come up with a decision."

"Can the maxim always answer ethical questions in such a simple manner?"

"No, not always—some of them can be very complex," I replied. "But at least it forms the basis for deliberating—it sets the guiding rules for the debate. At times it steers the parties to seek the proper information for the continuation of the debate. That is all that a general moral principle is expected to do. The rest is human judgment."

We had completed a circle around the lake so we decided to take a break. We sat down on a park bench near where the black swans were swimming gracefully.

"Can you illustrate the application of your moral principle with some less blatantly evil act—say stealing or fornication?"

"I could, but I will stay with killing. It is a dandy for discussing moral dilemmas."

"I thought that we had exhausted it."

"Not by any means. What about suicide? What about abortion? What about euthanasia or mercy killing? What about the death penalty? These have been and will continue to be mammoth moral issues for years to come. In addition, science is creating moral dilemmas so rapidly that the high priests are finding it difficult to keep coughing up new and improved edicts. Cloning is the newest case in point [68]."

"OK, what about suicide? How do the Christian and your Neo-humanism views compare on the issue?"

"I am not going to continue to compare the philosophy of life presented here to existing religions. I think that I have already demonstrated that their moral codes are arbitrary, inconsistent, confusing and flawed."

"OK, just discuss it from your point of view. Is suicide morally justified?"

"Suicide—the killing of one's self—is still a killing of a human being. Since it reduces the population by one member, it hurts the mission and it is wrong—unethical. There are, however, exceptions to this general statement, as for example when someone kills himself to protect or save others."

"Can that ever be the case other than in a war situation?" Estelle wondered.

"Yes, it can. People sacrifice themselves daily around the world during earthquakes, floods, tsunamis, hurricanes, fires, shipwrecks, etc., to protect others, especially children. We also have cases where an incapacitated person becomes such a burden to his family that he decides to commit suicide to save them from financial ruin. This act could be justified as moral—the overall mission may be served in the balance. But the key is that each case has to be analyzed—the act can be both moral or immoral depending on its effect on the mission."

We got up from the bench and started on our second walk around the lake.

"What about euthanasia?" Estelle inquired.

"Same story here, another act of killing that would be judged on its effects on the mission. It usually occurs when someone is in unbearable physical pain due to some debilitating disease, and his own mission is totally abandoned. He (or she) is very incapacitated and unable even to commit suicide. Helping him die is viewed as an act of mercy. Whether it helps the mission or not would depend on the specific case. I can also envision a lot of morally *neutral* cases here—the suicide having no effect on the overall human mission."

"Really? How so?"

"If the person is alone in the world, quite old and unable to pursue his mission any longer, the effects of the act is like normal death due to old age. Many of these people would have died anyway, if it weren't for science keeping them *artificially* alive. Of course, even if euthanasia is legalized,[12] care must be taken to ensure that there is no foul play. It must be positively ascertained that the person has indeed asked to be put to death—that he has no interest in continuing with his mission. Otherwise, it would be killing without mission-enhancing reasons, i.e. murder."

"I see. Can we next discuss abortion? Can you come up with a solution to the moral dilemma of abortion using your moral maxim?"

"The problem with abortion is that people do not agree on the time that the fetus becomes a person—a human being. The question

---

[12] The Netherlands legalized euthanasia in 2002.

is partly scientific, partly political and not really well understood. Once this has been settled, then from the time we consider the fetus a person, aborting is equivalent to killing. And we have discussed killing extensively above—it can be moral or immoral depending on the circumstances."

"Can you think of reasons why one would kill a fetus even after the date the fetus is acknowledged to be a human being?"

"If you stretch your imagination you might come up with cases where abortion may be justifiable even then—again it has to do with serving the mission in the balance. I can envision a case where a widowed mother may die from the birth and she already has five children who depend solely on her for their upbringing, etc."

"I see. Can you also discuss the death penalty vis-à-vis your maxim? Do states have the right to kill one of their citizens? A lot of the criticism comes from people who claim they do not!"

"The killing by anyone (including the state) is morally justified only if it can be shown that such an act aids the mission. Arguing about the rights of the state diverts the issue from a moral one to a political one."

"Do you think that executing a perpetuator of a heinous crime aids the mission?"

"Again, it would depend on the circumstances—you must examine how it effects the mission. In a very poor country where children are dying of starvation, the cost of keeping the criminal incarcerated humanely for a lifetime may not be warranted—the mission may be better served by executing him. In the richer western societies, the moral balance would be with the death penalty if it can be shown conclusively that it is a deterrent—that it discourages other criminals from killing in the future. Criminal experts appear to disagree on its value as a deterrent, which means that there has been no conclusive study on the issue up to the present. So that is where we should concentrate our efforts and not on interminable discussions on the rights of the state, the sanctity of life, religious objections based on patriarchical edicts and the like."

"Do you think the maxim will withstand the test of time? How well will it handle dilemmatic moral issues created by future scientific advancements?"

"No differently than present issues—you put them up to scrutiny on their effects on the mission."

"You already mentioned cloning. How do you handle that? It, too, involves killing some embryo, doesn't it?"

"You want me to analyze the morality of cloning?"

"Yes," she responded with alacrity.

"But it's a rather complex issue—I am not even sure I understand all its scientific aspects. The analysis may be entirely superficial."

"Do it anyway, not as an authoritative moral analysis but as another demonstration of the applicability of your moral maxim," Estelle insisted.

"How much of the science of cloning do you know?" I asked.

"Aside from what I already said—the possible embryo killing—about as much as anyone can know from reading Ira Levin's *The Boys from Brazil*," [69] she replied laughing. "I still get this spine-chilling feeling when I think about all those cloned Hitlers."

"That's probably the source of knowledge of all its vociferous opponents," I replied, also laughing.

"To begin with," I started, "as of today, there are two types of controversial cloning [68,70-72]. The first, called *Nuclear Replacement,* produces a duplicate of an existing being by starting with an embryo, removing its DNA and then replacing it with the DNA from the adult being. It has been used to produce duplicate sheep—notably Dolly. The second is called *Therapeutic Cloning.* It is the same technique, but now the original DNA is replaced with DNA from an adult being who suffers from an incurable disease. Then the embryo's stem cells are removed and then—hopefully—used to create tissue or some new healthy organ for transplantation back into the sick being that supplied the DNA. The process grows an organ that is not rejected by the recipient, but the embryo dies in the process. That's a very brief explanation of the two controversial techniques. There are some other variations on therapeutic cloning that do not involve embryos, but they are not controversial, nor are they very effective."

"Fine. Now apply your maxim. What do you get? Are they ethical or not?"

"Well, do any of them cause harm to the mission? In my opinion, no! Do any of them aid the mission? Yes, categorically so, especially therapeutic cloning which has the potential of helping thousands to survive and complete the remainder of their missions."

"Let's be more specific. What about this nuclear replacement—the creepy technique that leads to carbon copy type human beings?"

"It's interesting that this statement is made by people who in any other context maintain that the environment (nurture) is responsible for our persona. In cloning, it somehow becomes all genetic."

"You don't think the cloned person will be a carbon copy of the donor?"

"I doubt it. You may be able to duplicate the genetic make up, but you cannot duplicate the donor's previous physical environment—the womb, the food and its chemicals, and all the other possible exposures to radiations and chemicals that effect the brain and thus the personality. So the likelihood is that even with identical genetic coding the individual will be unique, like in cases of identical twins. We will never know for sure if it becomes outlawed before it is performed, will we?"

"What if it turns out that it is a carbon copy?"

"Even then, I can't find anything inherently immoral about it—I can't see how it can negatively effect the mission. On the other hand, I can think of many ways that the result could help the mission, and thus it would be moral to allow it."

"Can you name one?"

"Certainly. A married couple loses their one-year-old child in a freak accident. Cloning could give them back their child—one year younger."

"It is amazing how easily you come up with examples that support your arguments but draw blanks when they don't."

"You are right, and that's why I think cloning should be allowed on a case by case basis like abortion,"[13] I replied. "Actually, the arguments against therapeutic cloning are the same as against

---

[13] The U.S. House of Representatives voted to ban human cloning in the summer of 2001. The U.S. Senate never took up the issue, so it never became law.

abortion; that the embryo—in this case a ball of cells without even a rudimentary nervous system—is a human being."

"But you disagree?"

"Considering the potential good it can bring to the human mission [73], it would be immoral not to pursue therapeutic cloning. Disallowing a potential benefit to the mission is equivalent to harming the mission," I said emphatically.

"But why do religions oppose it?"

"I have already stated that I will no longer critique their reasons. Most of their pronouncements are contradictory, vague and unconvincing—easily rebutted even by a free-thinking novice."

Estelle remained silent for a while. We had now walked around the lake twice—a total distance of nearly two miles. We were starting to tire and stopped at a coffee shop for a cup of cappuccino and some biscotti.

"What about moral dilemmas involving self-survival vs. collective survival?"

"You mean running away to save your own life rather than fighting the enemy to protect your country?"

"Yes."

"I think that in such cases, personal survival yields to collective survival, i.e. sacrificing yourself is noble and good—running away, craven and bad. Between two moral acts the one contributing more to the mission has the edge. It is pretty obvious that the survival of many is more vital to the mission than the survival of one. Societies already recognize this rule and encourage it, awarding those that make the right choice with 'hero' status, as we noted earlier when we discussed suicide. Our maxim explains the whole thing away very nicely," I ended, gloating.

Secondary Ethics

Estelle was visibly irritated about the gloating.

"OK," she said, "I think we have exhausted moral dilemmas that involve death. What does your maxim do in judging some other acts like discrimination, divorce, homosexuality, pornography, stealing, lying, fornicating, etc?"

"Let's start with discrimination—it is readily dispensed with," I replied. "The use of race, ethnicity, creed, etc. as a justification for obstructing someone's pursuit of mission is blatantly immoral—it is in direct conflict with the maxim. One can usually come up with scenarios that turn nearly every human act from moral to immoral—including killing as we already noted. But discrimination may well be the exception to this rule. Personally, I haven't been able to imagine a circumstance where this act becomes moral," I added with a tone of finality.

Estelle remained silent indicating solid agreement.

"Next we move to divorce," I continued. "Without children, I think it is morally neutral—maybe even ethical. If both parties agree to part their paths, divorce allows them to pursue a fresh cycle of the procreative aspect of their mission. If there are young children and there are no dangers in staying together, divorce should be considered immoral. The mission is better served in the balance if the partners stay together and parent them until the children are mature enough to absorb the divorce experience."

"Is it ever unquestionably ethical?"

"Yes, when one of the two partners is abusive, the other family members could be seriously harmed. In such cases religions that forbid divorces routinely refuse to accept moral responsibility for the unpleasant results. Our maxim here leaves no room for wavering in such cases."

"What about pornography? Most religions condemn it as evil. How is it viewed under the prism of your maxim?"

"Most pornography, I think, is morally neutral—I can't personally see how it hurts anyone's mission. Child pornography is certainly evil—doubly so. It encourages abusive behavior towards children and at the same time children are actually being abused in creating it. But I must stress that we are discussing morality here and not legality, which should be decided by democratic due process."

"You know, one of the most fascinating and morally confusing human acts is lying [78,79]. I often catch myself lying, and I am not always certain whether it was ethical or unethical. Could you analyze lying vis-à-vis your moral maxim?"

"Certainly. You don't really have to be very imaginative to come up with examples that show lying to be moral, reprehensibly immoral or morally neutral. The key is always to ascertain the effects that the lying has on someone's life mission."

"How about some illustrations of immoral lying?"

"Easy. Committing perjury and getting away with murder is obviously an immoral act. A life has been stopped from pursuing the mission and the murderer is still at large, threatening more mission stoppages. Lying under oath and sending an innocent person to the gas chamber is a similar act—one of the original ten commandments if I am not mistaken. Immoral but less reprehensible would be lying about qualifications to gain a career advantage. It obviously obstructs a more deserving person's assent to his legitimate maximum potential."

"What sort of lying is ethical? Can you think of some examples?"

"Dozens of them, but there is no need to bore the reader. What of lying to a disadvantaged child about his success on a task, to urge him to continue? What about lying to a seriously injured person about his condition to encourage him to fight for his life? Both acts result in aiding a person's pursuit of life and mission and cause no harm to anyone else."

"I see. Can you quickly think of some morally neutral lies—*white lies* as they are often called?"

"Yes, certainly. The existence of Santa Claus is a lie—a conspiracy of lying—that involves the entire nation with no harmful results on anyone's mission. The tooth fairy, monsters, witches, and Disney characters are similar lies as well. I personally lie often to annoying telemarketers who insist that I have won a prized vacation, when all they want is to sell me some time-share unit. Women lie habitually about their age in social gatherings—always on the younger side. Men are notorious liars about their success with women and the stock market—about the great deals they struck in buying an automobile. No harm done to anyone's pursuit of mission, so the maxim proclaims such lies morally inconsequential. By the way, non-believers feel that the existence of god is also a lie and an immoral one at that—on the basis of the proposed non-believers moral maxim, of course. But I don't plan to re-start the religious disagreements here—I am remaining positive and I am continuing with the development of Neo-humanism."

"I am glad. Let's move on to stealing and fornicating then."

"OK. To begin with, society cannot function if stealing is condoned," I replied. "Chaos will ensue and people will not be free to pursue their missions. Fornicating can create doubts about the identity of the parents, and lead to child neglect—a mission negative. Thus they are both immoral, unless there are mitigating circumstances that could convert them to moral."

"What kind of circumstances could do that?"

"Well, what about stealing to feed a child dying of starvation? Or stealing a bomb from a group of terrorists ready to blow up a bridge during peak hour traffic?"

"OK, you are right, there are scenarios that could make stealing moral. Not legal, of course, just moral."

"No, not legal. But acquittal is possible under such circumstances—juries are often moved by such circumstances and use morality in their decisions."

"But what about copulating with your neighbor's wife? Don't tell me you can find circumstances that make even this—one of the commandments—moral?"

"Let me see," I answered. "Let's assume that an attractive female and her husband live next door and we are friendly with both of them. One day they come over and confide that their efforts to have a child have failed because of the husband's infertility. They request that I sleep with the attractive neighbor for a few times in the hope that she becomes pregnant. Would you refuse this desperate cry for help? Don't you think that the circumstances make this fornication moral?"

"I noticed you used the word attractive twice," she replied. "Let me turn the question around. Would you agree to it if she looked like Quasimodo[14]?"

"Never mind that," I replied. "Would you agree to it if I agreed to it?"

"No, I would not."

"You would deny them the opportunity to fulfill an important part

---

[14] Quasimodo was the hunchback of Notre Dame—a notably unattractive fellow.

of their mission? Why?"

"For two reasons. First, because it is against my principles—I am not bound by your maxim, you know. Second, I have another solution for their problem. I would send them to a sperm bank—they could try for a test tube pregnancy."

"There you are," I replied laughing. "It's not only the maxim that can resolve some of today's moral dilemmas. Advances in science can do it also."

Morally Neutral Acts

"Now could you elaborate on what you called morally neutral activities—the ones that are neither bad nor good?"

"Certainly. How about women priests, ministers, bishops, popes, patriarchs or whatever? What of dress codes for men or women, mandatory fasting, facing this way or that during prayers, designating the number of obligatory prayers per day, mandatory pilgrimages to *holy* places, forbidding women to drive or become professionals? I can sit here and make a huge list of activities that religions prohibit as evil, which don't seem to be even remotely related to the mission. In some cases—restricting women's pursuit of their maximum potential, for example—the forbidding itself is evil."

"What about homosexuality? Most religions consider the act unethical. Would you consider it morally neutral?"

"I think I would—the maxim would—I can't see where it might hurt or hinder the mission. Can you?"

"I don't know—I am not a Neo-humanist. But having sex with a person of the same gender does not seem to promote the mission. It could never lead to children, as you know."

"Yes, I do. But neither does swimming, mountain climbing or eating nuts. Homosexuals can pursue their missions and be moral in all other aspects, including raising children. They are condemned capriciously—there is no moral maxim around to help people decide."

We had started to walk towards the car now for the return home.

"It looks like you are very proud of your maxim—you had an answer to every question that I put to you," Estelle said. "Yet you remarked earlier that there are cases when the maxim falls short. Can you discuss some of those?"

"Yes, they usually involve actions whose effects on the mission are hard to predict—when the scientific information is incomplete."

"Do you have some specific examples?"

"Yes, I do. Should we drill for oil off the coast of Florida, or in some Alaskan wilderness? Should we bury our nuclear waste in some western desert or in the bottom of the sea? Should we use the water from a lake for farming or will it kill some endangered species of fish? As long as the results of such actions are not totally understood, they will remain dilemmas, solved primarily by politicians."

"I thought these environmental dilemmas were political issues, anyway," Estelle remarked.

"At present they are primarily political issues because religions have no moral maxims to deal with them. But under our moral maxim they are moral issues because they influence the overall mission. Likewise with issues of drinking, smoking and abusing drugs."

We had now reached home. I parked the car inside the garage and we both headed for the living room.

"Do you think this maxim of yours is going to change people's behavior?" Estelle asked in an obvious effort to bring closure to the issue. "If I recall correctly your main point of the *Good vs. Evil* dialogue (first chapter) was that all the existing religious moral codes have not changed people's immoral behavior—that's why we need laws, the police and countless other people. Do you think your maxim will do it?"

"What do you take me for—an idiot?" I replied. "If everyone adopted this philosophy of life, some of the existing moral confusion will be reduced. The time that's now wasted on debating moral dilemmas might also be reduced. But bring about a change in human behavior? Forget it. It would take a brain mutation from a cataclysmic event to do that!"

How Do We Find Happiness?

"Today, I am tackling the subject of how to find happiness and contentment in a life without faith," I told Estelle one morning while I was helping her set the breakfast table.

"Well," she said as she was pouring the coffee into the cups, "you ought to know what to write. You've always claimed to be a happy guy with no need for religion. But what do you mean by happiness—who understands the meaning of it, anyway?"

Estelle's question was legitimate, but going back and arguing about the definition of abstract concepts is not the way to start—it usually leads to a complete deterioration of the argument. I had to do something about the question, but I also had to stay on guard. Estelle would love it if she caused enough confusion to derail the book project.

"Why don't you look it up in a dictionary?" I replied.

She got up and picked up one (Funk and Wagnall's) and, a minute later, she started reading it out loud.

"It says here that happiness is *the state or quality of being happy.* Then it defines the word *happy* as *yielding or marked by happiness.* See? I told you. You are actually dealing with a circular concept—one that cannot be defined."

"Gimme that," I said and grabbed the dictionary away from her.

"Here. It gives more than one definition. It goes on to say that the word happy also means *enjoying, giving or indicating pleasure, joyous, or blessed.*"

"OK fine—it looks like it is synonymous to pleasure, then," she acquiesced. "Well, if you ask me, many things give people pleasure. I have also noted that they depend on a person's age. Happiness comes to a kid quite differently from the way it comes to an adult. Personally and for today, going shopping will provide me with some pleasure, so I am planning to do it right after breakfast. You can stay here and write about happiness all you want. I am going out there to experience it."

"Could you delay it for a half an hour or so? I would like to *use you* to introduce the topic."

"Me? How?"

"The way I see it—and plan to discuss it—there are two major types of happiness. The first and most important one is *long lasting happiness*—the sustained sense of satisfaction and contentment that lasts through a person's lifetime. The second one involves activities that bring happiness that are satisfying but short-lived. The pleasure derived from them is strong while one is engaged in the specific activity, but wears off as the activity wanes. You are a generally happy person, so I am hoping that you can help me to introduce this whole issue and more specifically the first category of happiness. Then you can go shopping."

"How can I help you? I don't even agree with the overall thesis of your book."

"It's quite simple, really. I am going to ask you a series of questions. If you answer them *honestly*, I think you will unwittingly utter the words I need—the proper introduction to my subject."

"Really? It sounds like a kid's game. Even if I do—which I doubt—what do you hope to gain from it?"

"Won't my argument be more convincing, if a devout Christian agrees with me? You might even change your mind and start espousing..."

"And what if you can't make me say what you want? I am quite adroit at these kinds of games, you know."

"Then I won't use it in the book," I answered cunningly. "But I am confident that this will work—just relax and answer the questions without attempting to *beat the game*."

"OK, I'll go along with it," she consented. "What are your questions? I don't have a lot of time. Edna is coming in about 20 minutes."

I got out of the chair and started pacing around, holding the coffee cup high up in the air. I paused for a few seconds to create an aura of mystery and apprehension, and then I fired the first question.

"Let's say you are on your deathbed, ready to depart the scene—this very minute. Is there anything you feel sorry about—anything you left undone? Do you feel *unfulfilled* in any way?"

"Well," she replied after thinking for a few seconds. "There is only one area of my life where I didn't go far enough—I didn't pursue it to my maximum potential."

"Was it your nursing career?"

"No, not that," she replied. "Nursing has been very pleasant, of course, and it has brought me many moments of contentment—helping people in distress is quite gratifying. Besides, if it wasn't for that, I might have never met you and…"

"Never mind that," I cut her off. "This is not a kiss-and-tell book. Which area did you mean then?"

"My painting," she replied. "I think I could have become a respected artist. My sister is—it runs on our side of the family. But I never really found the time to cultivate it."

"Perfect," I replied.

"Perfect?" she uttered, somewhat annoyed "I hesitantly acknowledged my lifelong unfulfilled dream and you mock me?"

"Sorry if it sounded like that. I meant perfect for my development here. But never mind that—let's get back to our little game. Let us consider now the same issue from the opposite optical angle. Of all the things you have accomplished in your life, which one is giving you a gratifying sense of fulfillment? Which one is giving you a sustained, long-lasting sense of happiness—the type you always claim to enjoy?"

"Can you make that a little clearer?" she asked.

"Get back to your deathbed, and try to imagine which specific event—or series of events—would have left you wanting, if you had missed it. Which one would have left you unfulfilled—caused you the biggest void if you left it undone? Which one would you make sure *not to miss*, if you came back to life for another go-round? Would it be the high school prom? Graduation from college? Getting your first job? Falling in love? Getting married? Joining the church? Serving the church? Serving the almighty? Which one?"

She sat there agonizing for quite some time.

"I think it is not a single event, but a whole series of them," she finally concluded. "It is this whole cycle of our life together. The falling in love, the dating, getting married, having children, raising them, being blessed with grandchildren—our whole family. I've met people without all this, and they seem anxious, desperate—a void in their eyes reflecting their empty hearts."

I had triumphed, but she didn't know it.

"Outstanding—thank you very much for your contribution," I said delighted. "My introduction to this section is now complete."

Estelle looked at me, puzzled.

"*My* contribution? What are you talking about?"

"My intended response to the question of *how to find lasting happiness is* 'by pursuing the activities of the proposed mission.' Your answers not only proved that I am right, it also formulated a kind of maxim for this type of happiness: *the amount of attained long-lasting happiness is directly proportional to the degree of success in the proposed mission.*"

"And how, pray, did my answers prove that?"

"Just examine your answer vis-à-vis the mission, and you will see exactly how. You are somewhat unhappy because you feel that you did not reach your maximum potential as an artist. This is the second item under primary contributions. In fact, it is also part of the first item in the second tier of the mission activities—the item on contributions to the culture. Your unhappiness of not reaching your maximum potential as an artist is compounded by the fact that you did not contribute much to the culture of the society—all your art has stayed within the family. On the other hand, you are very happy and contented, because you have completed—very successfully, I might add—the third item, that of marrying and producing your own offspring, grandchildren, etc. In fact, you are still engaged in this part as a grandparent, and thus you are still milking it in terms of happiness. Note also that nursing has brought you many moments of contentment—these are your own words—even though it was not your first career option. Nursing is one of the activities in the second tier of the mission—the part about medical professions."

"And where is God in this definition of happiness?" Estelle demanded to know.

"Wherever you put him in your answer. Nowhere, I guess. And that is where I need him to be in this development. The main thesis of the book is that he is not needed for the attainment of happiness—or anything else in our lives."

"But in all my answers, my activities are presumed to be within the context of my faith, they are performed in Jesus Christ, our Lord and Savior," she replied.

"I'll put that in the book, but I doubt that any of my readers would buy into this sort of gibberish," I replied.

Estelle looked somewhat baffled—bewildered. But I knew that her glazed look also meant that her mind was running at billions of brain operations per second, searching for ways to recover from the setback.

"OK, fine," she started, regaining some of her composure. "Answer me this, then. What about the romance, the love and affection, all the things that give us that warm, cozy feeling in life? Our marriage had all these and that's why it brought this lasting happiness. I don't see any of these mentioned in your outline of the mission."

"Oh, these feelings are there—of course they are. Nature put them there, as additional incentives. They are the reason why we are so enamored with these activities—why we pursue them like an addict pursues his fix. They are not, as some romantics suggest, ethereal happenstances emanating from the soul proving the nobleness and pathos of the human condition and the existence of a deity—that's verbal rubbish. So you see, we all seem to be *programmed to want* to do nature's work—our mission—and to experience happiness while we are doing it. That's precisely what happened to you, even though you don't subscribe to the mission."

There was a knock at the front door. It was Edna. Estelle picked up her purse and car keys and left without saying another word. I was now alone to pursue the topic without interruptions.

Let us return to our discussion of the first category of happiness. I am sure that it is hard to accept all this without some skepticism. So I would like you—the reader—to sit back in an armchair, relax, and go through the same exercise that Estelle went through. Assuming, of course, that you have lived long enough to have the appropriate experiences.

Try to think of the various times in your life when you experienced your utmost happiness. Try to dissect the reasons why you now have some lasting sense of satisfaction and contentment—the sensation that you didn't leave things unfinished.

I am pretty confident that the result will be the same as Estelle's. And if you are a generally unhappy person, it will turn out that your success in the mission has been wanting.

Just like there exist two tiers in the mission, so it is with happiness as well. The most satisfying and *lasting* happiness comes from engaging in the activities listed in the first tier of the mission. Activities in the second tier provide satisfaction that is short lived—it ends when the activity terminates. People engaged in the health or teaching professions experience this type of happiness—it gradually disappears after their careers end.

The farthest an activity is removed from the tasks of the mission, the lesser the degree of pleasure and happiness that it can provide. If the activity is unrelated to the mission, the attainment of happiness will remain elusive. And if it is against the mission, malaise might set in that may eventually lead to melancholy.

I am so convinced of all this that I am proposing that the word "happiness" can only be understood when placed in this context. In fact, I feel that happiness and activities that enable the species to grow and thrive are almost a tautology—that happiness and the proposed mission are intertwined and nearly indistinguishable.

The lists of activities that lead to the two proposed categories of happiness are outlined below. The parallels between the first category, and the mission proposed in the previous section are astonishing.

GENERAL STATEMENT ON HAPPINESS: *Lasting happiness is attained by successfully engaging in the activities of our mission in life.*

Activities that Lead to Sustained, Long Lasting Happiness

A. Individual acts of survival and successful pursuit of our maximum potential.

B. Falling in love, marrying, having children, parenting them properly, and then grand-parenting their children, thus helping all descendents to repeat the same cycle successfully.

C. Acts that aid in the defense of our nation (territory and culture), especially when under peril.
D. Contributions to the culture of the society, i.e. to such fields as literature, poetry, music, theatre, dance, other arts, etc.
E. Contributions to fields that improve the life of the members of the society such as science, medical professions, teaching professions, etc.
F. Philanthropic and altruistic acts toward the needy members of society.
G. Activities that safeguard and improve our cosmos—the preservation of our ecosystem—so that all life can flourish and evolve.

Activities that Provide Ephemeral Joys and Pleasures

A. Engaging in activities that provide pleasures specific to your age and your personality (playing with toys, games, sports, fishing, hunting, mental games, parties, social gatherings, shopping, etc.) *Matching your environment to your personality.*
B. Non-participatory activities involving mission activities (reading books, watching sports or movies and stage plays, attending concerts, art exhibits, weddings, etc.).

Let us elaborate a bit further on some of the activities belonging to the first category of happiness—sustained and long lasting. Their importance as part of our individual mission in life has already been discussed in a previous section. We should also stress that these activities, if successful, do not only bring happiness and contentment to the individual, they also bring happiness to the whole of society as well. For this reason they are blessed by society and often highly rewarded.

The first three are the major factors in long lasting happiness. The rest are activities that provide happiness whose strength gradually diminishes with the passage of time.

Let us consider the first item—raw individual survival in the face of adversity and reaching one's maximum potential.

During peaceful and prosperous times, survival is not a serious issue and people concentrate on the task of rising to their optimum potential. Success here brings enduring, long-term contentment and also facilitates success in all the other parts of the mission.

As we pointed out in the discussion of activities that promote the mission, reaching our maximum potential is difficult because we don't know what our potential is. Aside from the lack of offspring, failure here is the second most often mentioned reason for grief and even depression, especially in senior citizenry. A major problem is that humans are not capable of self-criticism—they lack the ability to comprehend their inadequacies and flaws. The old Socratian adage of *"know thyself"* has not become any easier with the passage of time. Not knowing one's potential often leads to failure and disappointment. I am not suggesting that people should not reach for goals that are beyond their capabilities—just that they should not dwell on their failures. They should move on and redefine their goals or concentrate on other parts of their mission.

The second item deals with the procreation process—the ultimate in the mission and thus in the pursuit of sustained happiness—happiness that lasts till the end of life. The optimum here is to go through the entire package successfully—erotic love, courting, marriage, parenting and grand-parenting. The natural urge to engage in this cycle is very strong. Nature constructed it that way to get us hooked—to ensure that we stay the course to the end of the procreation process.

Erotic love may be the epitome of happiness. Parenthood brings elation, bliss and joy. The glorious birth of a child is the zenith of activities in the mission of our existence It also brings a profound sense of accomplishment. It provides meaning and purpose to our lives. As we grow older, we watch our contributions to the species grow up with enormous pride. As long as our offspring are doing well, the sensations of happiness and fulfillment continue unabated. Their successful existence validates our own life. We have done our duty to aid our species not only to multiply but to flourish as well.

When a child arrives everyone is happy—the species has added to its population. The parents become heroes proudly exhibiting their contribution to the whole. Passersby stop to admire the child, pronouncing it cute and adorable. Old folks are especially enamored with babies. Their eyes reflect joy at the sight of one, especially if they were never blessed with one of their own. They share in society's happiness by leading the cheer for the new arrival. It gives them a renewed sense of belonging.

The connection of lasting happiness to the prescribed mission is apparent. We have already noted that religions attempt to extract credit for successes in this area, but refuse culpability when things go astray. Politicians and governments get in on the bandwagon also—laws that favor parents are always well received. Monetary rewards for producing offspring abound, from tax credits to actual cash. Some are meant to really help the species, others are only gimmicks for politicians to claim credit for the happiness and fulfillment of their constituents. Kissing babies during political campaigns is one of the most effective ways to pile on the vote.

I have met people whose only success in life was parenting a good child. Incredibly, this one success was enough to make them feel fulfilled. One man was an alcoholic, unable to hold a steady job and lived in the skid row—his wife long gone. Another had committed a crime and spent most of his adult life incarcerated. Yet another had been incapacitated by an accident, living his life in a wheelchair with very meager means and scant accomplishments. All these people had one thing in common, the rearing of a successful child. This single act of contribution to the species was sufficient to give each one of them gratifying and prolonged happiness.

We come now to the last aspect of the cycle of procreation—grand-parenting. The joys here are unparalleled. Many claim that the happiness enjoyed here is of a higher plateau that even that of parenting. The usual explanation is that grandparents enjoy the fun without the responsibilities. But it is a lot more than that. Becoming a grandparent heralds the completion of the ultimate part of the mission in life—procreation. This successful completion brings on a sense of perpetual happiness and continuous joy for the rest of one's days, even if all the other aspects of the mission ended up less than stellar. The pleasures of grand parenting have been so well advertised that every statement one can make is most likely a cliché.

The third item in this category deals with activities in the defense of one's country—both territory and culture. Though these activities are capable of bringing immense amounts of sustained and protracted happiness, they are not always available for participation. In times of peace such activities are totally absent, though societies often attempt to rally its people with artificially created replacements (war on poverty, wars on drugs, sports activities, etc.). In times of war, they are automatically elevated to a high priority, and they result in extreme and sustained happiness in the form of patriotic acts. Such acts can be major ones (actual participation in the fighting) or secondary ones (working in hospitals, munitions factories, contributing money to the war effort, rationing, even *flag-waving*). All these provide people—especially those who were unsuccessful in their other mission activities—with happiness of unsurpassed dimensions.

The irony here is that these activities are undesirable and desirable at the same time. Peace is desirable because it allows the nation to go about its main business of multiplying and prospering. But in the absence of war, the availability of patriotic activities is scant and their brand of happiness unavailable. One can easily understand why unscrupulous leaders create artificial wars that they can win. Happiness—in the form of patriotism—is elevated and the leader's popularity skyrockets. In the event of failure in such activities, the humiliation and shock are also unsurpassed, because the happiness/unhappiness takes on a *collective* nature.

The remaining activities listed there come from the second tier of the mission and the happiness they provide is less intense, and of shorter duration. Even so, they can be quite satisfying, and in the absence of success in activities of the first three items these can serve as very good substitutes.

Let us look briefly at philanthropic acts—acts directed towards the less fortunate members of society. Religions are strong advocates of such acts—they want their followers to consider them indispensable to their faith.[15] They hope that the joy derived from doing them will be attributed to the satisfaction of doing god's work—of following the church's dictates. But the resultant feelings of joy have nothing to do with faith. They are there because these activities are a part of the human mission.

The reader will recall that in the section on the human mission, philanthropy was defined as the act of helping the less fortunate pursue their respective missions. It was also noted there, that philanthropic acts need to be extended from addressing raw survival to helping others achieve their personal maximum potential. This will enable them to leave the ranks of the needy and to proceed to the rest of their mission on their own. In this section we contend that such an extension opens up new arenas of derivable happiness. There is much happiness to be derived—for example—from helping a student get his high school or university degree. There is much satisfaction to be gained by serving as a surrogate grandparent to a child who has none of his own. Mentoring orphans, helping disadvantaged children to master difficult tasks, even babysitting for working mothers are other activities that can be included in this type of philanthropy. And such activities do not only bring delight and joy to the philanthropists; they also result in lasting happiness to the beneficiary because they help him successfully complete a major part of his own mission.

It is worthwhile to take a brief look at activities that produce short-term pleasures—ephemeral type happiness. They are the ones outlined in the second list of the section. Those are strongly related to one's personality. Not everyone enjoys fishing or hunting, mental games or social gatherings. Optimum happiness here is achieved when the activities match one's character, both in the participatory and the non-participatory cases.

Sports represent a replacement—an imitation—for war, and they are especially popular in times of peace and prosperity. The feelings of happiness when one's team emerges victorious are so intense that

---

[15] Church officials keep shouting that their faith is "*about helping the widows and orphans.*"

they could lead to uncontrolled celebratory rioting. Conversely, the anguish of defeat is so devastating that it may lead to numerous sleepless nights—even an occasional heart attack. Incidentally, when real war breaks out, interest in sports wanes dramatically.

Books, movies and theatrical plays are quite popular and bring a lot of gratification—though it is rather short-lived. The most popular movies are about the first three groups of activities. Audiences never tire of romantic stories with a happy ending, because they want to see an important aspect of the mission successfully completed. War stories with good vs. evil themes are also well-liked themes—especially when good triumphs over evil at the conclusion. This means that we don't only extract happiness from engaging in the activities of the mission, we never tire of watching others engage in it as well. In fact, it is reasonable to enunciate the following maxim: *the degree of popularity an activity enjoys in books, movies, plays, etc., is proportional to the amount of sustained happiness it brings when successfully performed in real life.*

"I see that you have delegated shopping to your lowest form of happiness-producing activities, the short-lived type. I presume that is where participation in religious activities would be, as well, if you were addressing the faithful."

It was Estelle who had just returned from shopping and was scanning the last few pages of the manuscript.

"If it weren't so, you wouldn't need to keep shopping in perpetuity to rejuvenate the pleasure," I replied. "In addition, enjoying such activities is a personality trait. That is why I put it where I put them. Most of the items there are personality dependent. By the way, you are becoming rather predictable in your critical commentary of the religious content of the book."

"*Matching your environment to your personality*—very pompous phrase there. Whatever do you mean by that?"

"I'm glad you asked—I am dying to explain it."

"Fine, but don't go into any long arduous diatribe."

"Don't worry—I'll be pithy. To be free of daily angst, you must create an environment that is suitable not only to your optimum skills, but also to your personality. A talkative person should not become a mime. A non-believer should avoid living in a small city full of born again Christians or orthodox Jews. An introverted personality should stay away from being a TV talk-show host. A person who faints at the sight of blood should not pursue a career as a surgeon. That's what I meant. If your daily routine is stressful, your daily disposition may be dark and gloomy and activities of major pertinence to your mission may be postponed or ignored."

"I see," Estelle said still studying the pages. Can I still play around with some of your other contentions here? Can I ask some additional questions?"

"By all means."

"For starters, I get a lot of pleasure from eating a good meal and drinking a good red wine these days. Where does that fit in your profound pronouncements?"

"Both basic acts of individual survival. The same is true for the rest of our bodily functions—there is no need to list them all here. There is pleasure in all these acts—nature put it there to encourage us to perform them. No species is going to survive if its members refrain from eating, drinking, having sex and the rest of it."

"Now I have a general comment to make," Estelle announced. "I find it hard to believe that a deep, sophisticated thinker like you—according to your own assessment—believes in this rather simplistic approach to happiness. I've known people with children and grandchildren who are not happy. I have heard of decorated veterans of the Vietnam War who are languishing in mental institutions. Happiness must be much harder to attain than by following your simple recipe of *fulfill this or that mission and happiness is at your disposal.*"

"It seems to have worked for you, didn't it?" I reminded her. "And you have already suggested that it has worked for me at the start of the section. I know that it is hard to accept that there exist simple, succinct answers to life's seemingly complex questions. But sometimes they do—and they are staring us in the face."

"However," I continued, "I concede that there are people who have successfully fulfilled a major part of their mission, and yet they are unhappy, sad or depressed. But such exceptions always exist when you deal with complex organisms like humans. When I assert that this or that activity will make people happy, I always mean that it will make *the majority of people happy*, even within the specific group that I am addressing—non-believers in my case. In other words, all assertions are understood to be applicable to humans *in a statistical sense*, as scientists like to state.

"Let me give you an example, so that we are quite clear on this—I don't want you coming in again with some anecdotal evidence that disproves the theory. Let us say that I make the claim that *people* enjoy being present at weddings, *watching a couple begin a major part of their mission*. Well, quite obviously, not everyone does. There may be a previously jilted lover of the bride in attendance, the mother who thought her boy—the bridegroom—deserved better, a jealous older sister, an agoraphobic, someone with a migraine, and others with reasons to be unhappy during such a joyous event. But these exceptions do not undermine the truth of the original statement, because the statement is meant to be correct *in a statistical sense*. Generalizations about human beings can only enjoy this kind of correctness—that is the nature of the human beast."

Estelle appeared to be running out of steam

"May I have one last crack at your theory?"

"You can have as many as you want," I replied. "I welcome them as a test of its validity."

"Do you remember that towards the end of the previous section you made the claim that death is part of your mission in life even though you didn't include it in your summary?" she asked.

"Yes, I do."

"Well, in this section you are claiming that happiness and *the mission* are almost a tautology. What does all that say about death in your theory? Are we to attain some happiness when we die?"

"Yes, I believe so—death will be a pleasurable and blissful event. It will be so even for those that have totally flopped in their missions. They will experience sadness and bitterness as they approach death, but their actual dying experience will be happy. Success in this part of the mission is guaranteed and so is the temporary bliss it will bring. And by the way, all evidence so far seems to verify the accuracy of this conjecture. People who died and were revived by modern medical techniques have all recalled the instant of death as an ethereally joyful moment."

Estelle remained silent, so I got up for my closing arguments.

"In closing, I have some advice for you and your religious cohorts," I declared with a categorical finality. "Since you long for religion, participation in religious activities will bring you some joy—some degree of ephemeral happiness. But as you admitted at the start of this section, long lasting and enduring happiness comes from pursuing the major activities of the mission, not from worshiping some deity. That is the whole truth and anything else *cometh of evil*," I shouted, taking my leave with the time-honored biblical cliché.

Do We Need A Government?

We the people of the United States, in order to form a more perfect union, establish justice, insure domestic tranquility, provide for the common defense, promote the general welfare, and secure the blessings of liberty to ourselves and our posterity, do ordain and establish this Constitution for the United States of America.

Preamble to the U.S. Constitution

The State's Mission

"What made you decide to write a section on politics?" Estelle inquired one evening, while knitting a hooded sweater for one of our grandchildren.

"It's a section on government—the state—a very intriguing topic," I replied. "That's all people talk about besides ethics and etiquette," I added smiling.

"Oh, I know that most people blame the government for all their problems—when they are not blaming other people, of course. But does government really have much influence in our lives?"

"Yes, it does," I replied. "Think of it this way. All humans are out there trying to best fulfill their missions, in reference to their own societies. But it is not a path strewn with roses. There are enemies out there undermining their efforts to succeed. There are friends or acquaintances gunning for the same jobs, competing for the same mates, or promoting the interests of their families often to the detriment of yours. On top of all that, you have other countries creating problems that may interrupt your normal progress so that you can help defend the nation. Government comes in to play a role in all this, and understanding this role is advantageous for a successful completion of the Neo-humanist mission."

"But what about the code of ethics? Doesn't it resolve conflicts that arise in society's competitive arena?"

"Not in the real world," I replied. "Codes of ethics are great for armchair discussions on moral dilemmas—euthanasia, abortion, cloning, etc—and for judging other people's behavior. But when people are personally involved in a moral conflict, the tendency is to twist the interpretation of the code to suit one's personal interest. All humans are programmed to behave that way—it is the part of their mission that encourages them to survive at all costs."

"Is that why we need the government?"

"Precisely," I replied. "Primarily for that, and for a few other reasons."

"What other reasons?"

I got out of my desk chair, walked over to Estelle and showed her the start of the present chapter.

"Here," I said. "Read the Preamble to the U.S. Constitution. It describes concisely why our forefathers decided to create a state."

Estelle read it out loud and posed to reflect.

"It sounds to me as if they decided to create a government that would help them pursue their mission," she said. "Actually your mission—the Neo-humanist mission."

"Congratulations—that's an acute observation. And thank you for helping with my development. I knew that we would find some common ground in this section—that you would help me develop it without your usual belligerence."

Estelle looked pleased that I was seeking her help.

"To rephrase your remarks," I continued, "the authors of the Preamble created a state and granted it a precise mission. The state's mission is *to create the conditions that would help people pursue their mission.* I totally concur—they took the words right out of my mouth. I am adopting it as the state's Neo-humanist mission, as well."

I paused for a few seconds to indicate to Estelle that I considered the previous statement profound.

"That's nice of you, and rather clever, I might add," Estelle remarked. "First you reference the Bible for your human mission and now the U.S. Constitution for your state mission. I am starting to conclude that you are adding prestige by association—that you are actually seeking converts."

"I am not and you know it. I was planning to place the proposed human mission at the epicenter of a state's mission—it's in line with everything else I have done in this book. Then I noticed that our forefathers had substantially scooped me—by creating a state to protect the…Neo-humanist mission. It was a rather bizarre coincidence that had to be brought to light."

"Maybe our forefathers were Neo-humanists," Estelle remarked sarcastically.

"We can baptize them so posthumously and ex post facto, if you like," I replied laughing out loud.

"Let's now give the Preamble a closer scrutiny and identify additional common ground with Neo-humanism," I continued after my laughter subsided. "The first two items mentioned there are *to establish justice and insure tranquility.* We were just discussing the need for that—that morality alone could not resolve conflicts among humans. A big part of the state's mission is to ensure that such disagreements are resolved in a fair manner, and if crimes are committed, the guilty parties are punished. With a fair justice system, domestic tranquility is enhanced and people's chances of succeeding in their missions are elevated."

Again I paused, to allow Estelle to absorb the points.

"The other tasks assigned to the state in the Preamble are meant to augment people with the rest of the activities of the human mission. *Providing for a common defense* obviously addresses the issue of external threats and improves it by centralizing it. *Promoting the general welfare, securing the blessings of liberty and our posterity* are phrases that re-iterate the need to aid my proposed human mission. I didn't use those precise words in the mission statement, but the meaning is the same—perpetuate and prosper."

"Except for the word *liberty.* I don't remember you stressing liberty in your mission statement," Estelle remarked.

"All civil rights are necessary for the successful pursuit of the mission—but I don't personally consider them a part of the mission. Liberty also leads to *equal opportunity,* another concept the forefathers implied in the Preamble. But your comment is welcome because it reminds us that a democratic regime is best—that all other forms of government fall short in providing equal opportunity to all citizens in the pursuit of the mission."

"Now," I started again, after a brief pause, "I want you to look at the Preamble once again and tell me what you don't see there."

"What kind of a silly game is that? Thousands of things."

"You are right. But what I have in mind is so glaringly absent that I thought it might catch your eye. I mean the word, *god*. You don't see a reference to *god* anywhere there, do you?"

"No, there isn't. I did notice that, and that's another reason why I suggested that our forefathers might have been Neo-humanists. Do you find that important?"

"I find it extraordinary. Here's a bunch of predominantly religious people who are constituting a new nation and they never mention that they are doing so *under god*, or *in the name of god*, or *trusting in god*, or *inspired by the holy ghost*, or any of the other religious clichés. In fact, I don't think that they used the word *god* in any part of the constitution."

"So the constitution makes no reference to god, fine, I have no problem with that. Everyone knows of the separation of church and state in the United States—it is also guaranteed by the first amendment[16]."

"That's right—I am glad you mentioned it. In fact, the amendment goes farther than the Preamble and makes it prohibitive for the state to be involved in religious matters."

At this point I got up again and faked a look of profound self-importance.

"All in all then, a good government is by its inception a Neo-humanist's paradise. It is formed to support the book's proposed mission, and all associations with god or organized religions are disallowed," I declared, enunciating clearly every one of my carefully chosen words.

"I have to admit that in this case you are right. I am not sure I like it—I would have preferred a bit of religion thrown in there somewhere—but if it has to be that way, I can live with it."

"Well, I have some good news for you," I replied. "There is plenty of religion in the government—in violation of the amendment,

---

[16] The first amendment states: Congress shall make no law respecting an establishment of religion, or prohibiting the free exercise thereof; or abridging the freedom of speech, or of the press; or the right of the people peaceably to assemble, and to petition the government for a redress of grievances.

of course. After all, we know that the majority of the people—and thus of the lawmakers—are religious, and feel the same way as you do. They need a little phrase—a little symbol here and there—to satisfy their uncontrollable urges of religiosity and they have sneaked them into the government, anyway."

"I suppose you are going to point them all out next."

"You bet," I replied. "I don't want the faithful to think that we—the non-believers—do not notice them. We do and we don't like it. But we generally forgive it—acknowledging that it is all pre-programmed behavior in their *god part of their brain* [2]," I added sarcastically.

"Start pointing out the violations—as you called them—and stop the sarcasm." You said that this would be a section without pointed exchanges," Estelle reminded me.

"You are right, I am sorry," I replied. "OK, let's start with the famous Pledge of Allegiance, recited daily in all sorts of *public* places. What is that phrase *under god* doing there? The forefathers never mentioned it. It's my understanding that the original Pledge of Allegiance didn't have it—Congress inserted it in 1954. So what is it except the product of some fanatic lawmaker who rammed it through, knowing that the majority would acquiesce?"

"It is a harmless addition—an acknowledgment of the fact that...."

"Then," I continued refusing to acknowledge her justification, "we have the two Houses of our Federal Government and probably countless other State and Local Houses starting their daily sessions with a prayer, alternating from Muslin to Jewish to Christian and ignoring everything else. And what about the fact that a new President, Supreme Court Justices and most other major government officials are sworn in using some *holy* book? What about swearing in witnesses in courts using the phrase, *so help me god*? Or the fact that many public schools are now teaching creationism? Did you notice that some towns put up nativity scenes in front of public buildings during the Christmas holidays? I can sit here and outline a multitude of governmental actions or decisions that have crept into our life that make a mockery out of the Constitution. It is as if religious people in power are forever looking for ways to *cheat the amendment* and sneak religion into every facet of our lives."

"Nobody is complaining except you," Estelle remarked.

"Plenty of people are complaining about these things, but their voices are drowned out by the shrieks of the pious."

"But you are the legendary champion of such complaints. Heck, if I put a dime—nay, a nickel, a penny, any coin—away for every one of your complaints against religion, I would be a multi-millionaire by now."

"Coins? Yeah, thank you for reminding me," I replied. "And what is this phrase that is stamped on every one of our coins—*In God We Trust*? Is that not the most audacious affront to the Preamble and the Amendment? By stamping this phrase, the government is tacitly agreeing that god exists, openly favoring religions who believe in a single god."

Estelle said nothing for a while—pretending to concentrate on a difficult section of her knitting. She was looking intently at a magazine's directions and counting stitches on the sweater's shoulder. I thought this was an opportunity to end this part of the section and move on. I had made my points, anyway.

Morality And The State

Estelle came over holding a skein of yarn and handed it to me to stretch between my arms so that she can wind it into a neat ball. It was a ritual we do often when she is knitting, silently, sometimes without even looking at each other. This time she spoke.

"What about morality in the government? Is there such a thing?"

"There can be—Neo-humanism can actually define it pretty precisely. But before I explain how, I want you to ponder the situation and observe all the confusion that presently exists."

"What kind of confusion? Everyone asserts that we are a moral nation. Don't you agree?"

"Believers always insist that morality is only possible under god or within some religion. We have just agreed that our government is by inception non-religious. So the inevitable conclusion is that our government can not be moral."

"But the preponderance of the people in the government are religious, so their collective decisions must be moral," she insisted.

"Based on the morality of which religion? We are a multi-religious country. It is conceivable that every congressman belongs to a different religion. Some of them may believe in no god, others in one god, some in two or more, some others in satan, and some may even worship the souls of their dead ancestors. The end result is the paradox of having an institution formed to be religiously neutral, run by people who make decisions using their personal religious morality. If that is not confusing, then the Tower of Babel was a paragon of clarity."

"And how would your philosophy of Neo-humanism eliminate this confusion?"

"You will recall that after I defined the human mission, I used it to define human morality, right?"

"Right. Are you now going to use the state's mission to define the state's morality?"

"Precisely, I replied. *A moral act by the state is one that's in line with its mission—an act or decision that promotes the human mission. Otherwise it is immoral or morally neutral—the terms having the same meaning as before.*"

"Can you give an example of some moral acts by the state?"

"A law that abolishes slavery, income tax deductions for children, support for creative activities, the development of a strong defense force, high quality education, bills that aid the economy, insistence on equal opportunity for all, etc."

"Can you name some immoral acts?"

"Laws that discriminate against a specific ethnicity, race or religion, laws that discourage people from marrying and procreating, laws that violate people's civil rights, officially sanctioned corruption in the justice system, bribery, etc.—all violations of its mission to provide the proper environment for its citizens to pursue their mission."

"Are there any acts that are moral for individuals but immoral for the state?"

"Certainly—the missions are not the same, so neither is the resultant morality. Nepotism is an example that illustrates the point. If an individual hires his son in his private business, that's taking care of his family—part of his mission—and the act is moral. But if some state official can legally hire his incompetent son to a government position, then the state is sanctioning nepotism—an obviously immoral act because it blocks others from reaching their maximum individual potential."

"All your examples refer to governmental actions that effect its own citizenry. What about actions that effect people of other nations? Is there morality in foreign policy?"

"An excellent question," I marveled. "At present there is the usual confusion. Every country claims to have a *moral* foreign policy, but none of them explain what they mean by the term. Many countries are run by dictators or by oligarchies that consider any act that keeps them in power as moral. Many countries follow the morality of their state approved religion—and there is more than one of those. It is rather difficult to come up with a universally accepted morality under such conditions."

"Could you eliminate the confusion by applying the theory of Neo-humanism?"

"Let's analyze the situation. Let's assume that all countries are democratic and all have adopted the Neo-humanist mission for their governments. Their morality would be automatically defined—moral acts would be those that aid their citizens in the pursuit of their missions. Are you with me so far?"

"Yes, I am."

"The troubles with this scenario begin when countries have conflicting interests. Democratic governments are responsible to their own constituencies—they have to keep them happy to stay in power. So they concentrate on issues that are moral from the internal point of view, but which could cause conflicts with other nations."

"Can you give an example of such an issue?"

"Certainly. Neighboring nations could clash over disputed territory that contains oil, or over the water of a river which is being polluted by one and used for drinking by the other."

"What is to be done then?"

"You will recall that even within a specific nation morality alone could not resolve moral dilemmas—individuals view morality from their own optical prisms. Do you recall what was additionally needed to resolve such dilemmas and avoid a societal chaos?"

"The formation of the state, right?"

"Precisely."

"Can't we do the same in the world scene? Can't we create a state over all states—a sort of federal world government—whose mission would be to create the proper conditions for nations to peacefully pursue their individual missions?"

"We could, but don't expect it to happen anytime soon. The United Nations is a half-hearted attempt to do that with the assortment of political regimes that we have today, but it is quite ineffective because it cannot enforce its decisions."

Estelle remained silent, and I had come to the end of my development.

"Besides," I added, "there are always one or more super-power nations around that prefer the present situation, because they control it. Whatever they do, they pronounce it moral. They certainly don't want some impartial body deciding otherwise. In conclusion, euphemistic phrases cannot camouflage the fact that in the world arena, morality is arbitrary and the law of the jungle still rules supreme."

EPILOGUE

"You know, I am so used to you arguing about the lack of logic in religious beliefs, the first part of the book is no real surprise. But how did you ever come up with such a simple yet meaningful philosophy of life?"

"You are starting to think that I might be right?"

"I like the succinctness of the thing. Our mission is to propagate the species. Activities that do that are ethical and bring on long lasting happiness. And the state's major function is to promote this mission. It all sounds like a simple yet powerful mantra."

"Yes, I know. No need to study a fat book and try to make sense out of its contradictory propositions. And the best part is that you don't have to worship anything or build temples to anyone—heck, you don't even have to *believe* in it. Think of it as a way to understand human existence—a guide on pursuing happiness under a sound moral code. As a bonus, it also provides guidelines for judging the effectiveness of the government."

It was a beautiful evening and we had just sat down to dine at a swanky Orlando restaurant. As soon as she asked the question, a familiar scene flashed through my mind. The scene was at the end of every Perry Mason movie. Perry Mason and his staff are sitting around a restaurant table and he would always be asked to explain what tipped him—how he managed to solve the mystery and apprehend the real culprit. Here I was also asked to explain how I succeeded in solving this perennial mystery of human existence.

"I'd really like to hear how you did it—how it came to you," she persisted. "Especially the latter part. I can guess how the definition of the mission came about—you even referred to the Bible on it. Besides it doesn't differ all that much from the Christian mission, except for the fact that we believe in God and accept Jesus Christ as our Lord and Savior. But how did you realize that the activities of the mission actually define *good,* and bring on happiness?"

This is bizarre, I thought. Even the way Estelle posed the

question was reminiscent of the Perry Mason scene. She had put it matter-of-factly, without belligerence—just the way Perry Mason's secretary would do it. Could it be that Estelle was becoming a Neohumanist? No, no way—we all know that's impossible. Could it be that the same Perry Mason scene had flashed through her mind and she was going along playing the secretary's part to humor me?

I took the airs of the celebrated detective and started on my explanation.

"It is more than just a theory, you know. It has a natural...truth in it. But before I explain, let me ask you this. What are some basic things that all people enjoy doing day in and day out as they go through life? A clue is what we are doing right now."

"Eating, drinking, sleeping, let me see..."

"Having sex?"

"I guess so."

"That was the first thing I noticed—nothing profound, mind you—but a clue, nevertheless. That, however we got here, the first three most pleasurable things we do—eat, drink and sleep—are necessary for our personal survival, and the fourth—sex—for our collective survival as a species. Are you with me so far?"

"Yes!"

"My next move was to generalize the idea *and turn it into an if and only if condition*, as the mathematicians are fond of saying. That *if an activity is pleasurable it serves survival, and if it serves survival it is pleasurable*. It wasn't just a whim, you understand—it made sense too. If I were to create a bunch of creatures and put them in a big plantation, this would be the first property I would bestow on them to enhance their chances of survival."

"Did that turn out to be true?"

"For most people, yes. There are some exceptions. It isn't true for a rapist or serial killer, for example—what they enjoy doing hurts the species—but for normal people, it is. It is true in a *statistical sense*, as we discussed earlier. The fact that activities that aid survival bring pleasure is easy to prove, as we saw. The other way around—how a given pleasurable activity helps the species—is not always obvious, but a little thought brings that out too. That was the case with the writing of a book, if you recall. You were initially appalled at my claim that it aids survival, but you eventually saw that it does, right?"

"Right."

"Next, I looked at *good and evil* and how it relates to the mission. I was astonished to notice that what we all—faithful and freethinkers alike—perceive as *good* are the activities I had included in the mission. And the opposite held for the *bad*."

"You mean that all humans perceive good and evil similarly? Without exceptions?"

"Oh, well, yes, there was some exception, usually on issues that are morally neutral. Some societies—usually theocratic—define pleasure sex as evil, others enforce fasting rules, some classify dressing in certain ways a sin, etc. But we seem to agree on the important things, and it makes perfect sense, of course. If we were programmed to pursue these activities to survive, and feel pleasure in doing them, the obvious thing would be to view them as good. Otherwise we would become mentally confused and society would implode."

"Is that why you feel that there is a natural truth in your proposals?"

"Yes. If our brains are programmed to pursue this mission, then I am not proposing a new mission, *I am just revealing our true mission.*"

"Amazing! Do you think you were somehow anointed by a higher force to dig it out?"

"Nice try," I said laughing. "But I am not the only one putting forth such notions, you know. Go to the references and read some modern thinkers [28-30, 45-48] and you will be surprised how often they keep coming up. All I did was put together a unified theory—a useful philosophy of life readily understood and easily practiced."

"By the way," I continued, "what's up with you today? You sound as if you are starting to come around. You are not thinking of becoming a Neo-humanist, are you?"

"Well, I've been wanting to, but my religiosity gene won't let me."

The end

REFERENCES AND NOTES

1) Aris P. D'Avenal, *"The Gene Conspiracy or Sorry...The Genes Made Me Do It,"* CD ROM (e-book), Deep South Publishing Co., Jan. 15, 2000. Published as a paperback by Writers Club Press, December 2000.

Notes: The author introduces the axiom entitled *Genes and the Survival Principle (GSP)* which states that; a) human behavior and personality traits are dictated by genes and b) all *Universal type Behavior* exists for the better survival of the species. A religiosity gene is postulated here and discussed right along with genes for patriotism, altruism, racism, etc. The notion of the *genal* condition is also postulated here for the first time, which explains excessive acts in survival.

2) Mathew Alper, *"The God Part of the Brain: A Scientific Interpretation of Human Spirituality and God,"* Rogue Press, May 2001.

Notes: The author argues that genes dictate not only physical characteristics of a species but *universal behavior* as well. He postulates a location in the brain (his God part), where spiritual cognitions, sensations and behaviors are generated.

3) Shankar Vedantam, *"Tracing the Synapses of Our Spirituality, Researchers Examine Relationship Between Brain and Religion,"* Washington Post, Sunday, June 17, 2001.

Notes: A review of University research on the religious pre-wiring of the brain.

4) Rhawn Joseph, *"Transmitter to God: The Limbic System, the Soul, and Spirituality,"* University Press, California, August 2001.

5) Andrew Newberg, M.D. et all, *"Why God won't go away: Brain Science and the Biology of Belief,"* Ballantine Publishing Group, April 2001.

Notes: Here are some phrases from the book that describes it pretty well: "In other words, mystical experience is biologically, observably, and scientifically real.....Gradually, we shaped a hypothesis that suggests that spiritual experience, at its very root, is intimately interwoven with human biology."

6) Larry J. Siever and William Frucht, *"New View of Self: How*

Genes and Neurotransmitters Shape Your Personality, and Your Mental Health," Diane Publishing Co., September 1999.

Notes: The book raises the issue of the biological origins of mental health. It concludes that we need a clearer understanding of the brain's dysfunctional mechanisms.

7) Deepak Chopra, *"How to Know God : The Soul's Journey into the Mystery of Mysteries,"* Three Rivers Press, February 20, 2001.

Notes: The author—a spiritual man—states that *"our brains are hardwired to find God."* Thus he agrees with the premise that religiosity is in the brain. What he does with this next, is quite interesting.

8) Terry Burnham and Jay Phelan, *"Mean Genes: From Sex to Money to Food: Taming our Primal Instincts,"* Penguin, August 2001.

9) Bertrand A. Russell, *"Why I'm Not a Christian, and Other Essays on Religion and Related Subjects,"* Simon and Schuster, 1977.

Notes: A classic in discussing the logical inconsistencies of Christianity. Must reading for non-believers of all shades and graduations.

10) S. Acharia, *"The Christ Conspiracy: Greatest Story Ever Sold,"* Adventures Unlimited, September 1999.

Notes: The author presents historical evidence that Christianity and Jesus Christ were created by members of various secret societies, mystery schools and religions, in order to unify the Roman Empire under one state religion.

11) Ruth H. Green, *"The Born Again Skeptic's Guide to the Bible,"* Freedom from Religion Foundation Press, 1999.

12) Peter C. Hill, Ralph W. Hood, Eds. *"Measures of Religiosity,"* Religious Education Press, July 1999.

13) Leonard C. Moffitt, *"Religiosity: A Propensity of the Human Phenotype,"* Nova Science Publishers, December 1997.

14) T. K. Desikachar et al, eds., *"The Social Context of Religiosity,"* University Press of America, January 1980.

15) Maurice De Bona, Jr., *"Atheist Reality and the Brain-Year 2000 Update,"* Desserco Publishers, November 2000.

16) Rueben E. Abel, ed., *"Humanistic Pragmatism: The*

Philosophy of F. C. S. Schiller," The Free Press New York, 1966.

Notes: Schiller fashioned a self-titled 'humanism' that gave special priority to the individual consciousness and free will for theorizing on the true, the good and the right.

17) F. C. S. Schiller and Warren E. Steinkraus, *"Mind: A Unique Review of Ancient and Modern Philosophy,"* University Press of America, October 1983.

18) Paul Kurtz, *"Humanist Manifesto 2000: A Call for a New Planetary Humanism,"* Prometheus Books, February 2000.

19) Noam Chomsky, *"The New Military Humanism."* Common Courage Press, July 1999.

20) Paul Kurtz, Ed., *"Sidney Hook: Philosopher of Democracy and Humanism,"* Prometheus Books, June 1992.

21) Percy B. Shelley, *"The Necessity of Atheism,"* Bodleian Library, December 1997.

22) Andrew Pyle, ed., *"Agnosticism: Contemporary Responses to Spencer and Huxley,"* Books International, Inc., August 1998.

23) Judith Hayes, *"A Happy Heretic,"* Prometheus Books, June 2000.

24) Gordon Stein, Ed., *"Encyclopedia of Unbelief,"* Prometheus Books, June 2000.

25) Peter A. Angeles, Ed., *"Critiques of God,"* Prometheus Books, January 1976.

26) Massimo Pigliucci, *"Tales of the Rational: Skeptical Essays about Nature and Science,"* Atlanta Freethought Society, May 2000.

27) Holmes Rolston, *"Genes, Genesis and God: Values and Their Origins in Natural and Human History,"* Cambridge University Press, March 1999.

Notes: The author concludes that religion does have a survival value for humankind and is not in any way incompatible with genetics or evolutionary theory. I agree.

28) Holmes Rolston, III, and Dave Garrison, *"Biology, Ethics and the Origin of Life,"* Wadsworth Publishing Co., September 1999.

29) Holmes Rolston, III, *"Environmental Ethics: Duties to and Values in the Natural World,"* Temple University Press, December 1987.

30) Don E. Marietta, *"For People and the Planet: Holism and*

Humanism in Environmental Ethics," Temple University Press, December 1994.

31) Richard L. Sturch, "*The New Deism: Divine Intervention and the Human Condition*," St. Martin Press Inc., October 1990.

32) Peter M. Rinaldo, "*Atheists Agnostics and Deists in America*," Dorpete Press, August 2000.

33) James A. Herrick, Thomas W. Benson, eds., "*The Radical Rhetoric of the English Deists*," University of South Carolina Press, November 1997.

34) William R. Stephens, "*An Account of the Growth of Deism in England*," *AMS Press*, April 1995.

35) Kerry S. Walters, "*American Deists: Voices of Reason and Dissent in the Early Republic*," New Library Press, June 2001.

36) Merrilee H. Salmon et al, eds., "*Introduction to the Philosophy of Science*," Hacket Publishing Co., January 2000.

37) Anthony O'Hear, "*Introduction to the Philosophy of Science*," Oxford University Press, September 1990.

38) Edwards, Paul, "*The Cosmological Argument*," in D. Burtill, ed., "*The Cosmological Argument*," Doubleday, 1967.

39) **Note:** Arnold Sadwin, M.D., ex-Chief of Neuropsychiatry at the University of Pennsylvania, (Who is Who of Science, 1995; of Medicine 1996) wrote the following in an amazon.com review of reference 2. *"For years, I have studied cases of people who suffered from varying degrees of head injury in which the victims showed radical changes in their religious behavior after their accidents. Though I was intrigued by this particular phenomenon, I could never really make sense of it until I read this book."*

40) Ed Viswanathan, "*Am I a Hindu? The Hinduism Primer*," Halo Books, August 1992.

41) Linda Johnsen, "*The Complete Idiot's Guide to Hinduism*," Macmillan Publishing USA, October 2001.

42) Daisetz Teitaro et al, "*An Introduction to Zen Buddhism*," Grove/Atlantic, Inc., May 1976.

43) Steve Hagen, "*Buddhism Plain and Simple*," Broadway Books, December 1998.

44) H. Byron Earhart, Ed., "*Religious Traditions of the World: A Journey Through Africa, North America, MesoAmerica, Judaism,*

Christianity, Islam, Hinduism, Buddhism, China and Japan," HarperCollins Publishers, Inc., July 1992.

45) Matt Ridley, *"Origins of Virtue: Human Instincts and the Evolution of Cooperation,"* Viking/Penguin, March 1998.

Notes: The author, a zoologist, attempts to resolve the contradictions between self-interest and mutual aid.

46) Jane Maienschein and Michael Ruse, eds., *"Biology and the Foundation of Ethics,"* Cambridge University Press, March 1999.

Notes: A collection of articles written by leading experts on the question on whether our moral principles can be related to our biological nature.

47) Richard D. Alexander, *"The Biology of Moral Systems,"* Aldine de Gruyfer, January 1987.

Notes: Early attempt to relate in using evolutionary concepts in the analysis of human behavior and ethical problems.

48) William A. Rottschaefer, *"Biology and Psychology of Moral Agency,"* Cambridge University Press, February 1998.

Notes: The author attempts to relate recent findings (1998 vintage) in biology and psychology to ethics.

49) Richard Leakey, *"Origins of Humankind,"* HarperCollins Publishers, August 1996.

50) John D. Barrow, *"The Origin of the Universe,"* Basic Books, May 1999. **Notes:** Modern cosmology. Theories of time, space, cosmic holes, etc., including the big bang theory.

51) Richard Ellis, *"Aquagenesis: The Origin and Evolution of Life in the Sea,"* Viking Penguin, October 2001.

52) Richard Fortey, *"Life: A natural History of the Four Billion Years of Life on Earth,"* Random House, Inc., September 1999.

53) Stephen W. Hawking, *"Brief History of Time: From the Big Bang to Black Holes,"* Bantam Books, Inc., September 1998.

54) Kenneth C. Davis, *"Don't know Much About the Universe: Everything you Need to Know About the Cosmos but Never Learned,"* HarperCollins Publishers, September 2001.

55) *"The Holy Bible: King James Version (KJV) with Concordance,"* World Bible Publishers, March 1988.

Notes: A misnamed book. Not much holy about all the massacres, rapes, betrayals, etc. portrayed in the old testament.

56) Eugene G, D'Aquilli and Andrew B. Newberg, "*The Mystical Mind: Probing the Biology of Religious Experience*," Fortress Press, August 1999.

57) James B. Ashbrook, Carol R. Albright and Anne Harrington, "*The Humanizing Brain; Where Religion and Neuroscience Meet*," Pilgrim Press, October 1997.

58) Gerald Hausman, ed., "*The Kebra Nagast: The Book of Rastaferian Wisdom and Faith from Jamaica and Ethiopia*," St. Martin's Press, Inc., October 1997.

59) Hugh Joseph Schonfield, "*The Passover Plot*," Element Books, February 1986.

60) John D. Crossan, "*Historical Jesus: The life of a Mediterranean Jewish Peasant*," HarperCollins Publishers, March 1993.

61) Desmond Morris, "*The Naked Ape: A Zoologist's Study of the Human Animal*," Random House, Inc., May 1999.

62) Kathryn Kindskoog, "*Fakes, Frauds and Other Malarkey: 301 Amazing Stories and How not to be Fooled*," Hope Publishing House, April 1993.

63) Harry Hoodini, "*Miracle Mongers and their Methods: A complete Expose*," Prometheus Books, February 1993.

64) Arthur K. Shapiro et al, "*Powerful Placebo: From Ancient Priest to Modern Physician*," The Johns Hopkins University Press, January 2001.

65) Lolette Kuby, "*Faith and the Placebo Effect: An Argument for Self Healing*," Origin Press, October 2001.

66) James Alison and Sebastian Moore, "*The Joy of Being Wrong: Original Sin through Easter Eyes*," Crossroad Publishing Co., June 1997.

67) Henn Blocher, "*Original Sin: Illuminating the Riddle*," Intervarsity Press, January 2001.

68) "*Bush States Claim Against All Cloning of Humans*," The Orlando Sentinel, page A3, April 11, 2002.

Notes: After conferring with religious leaders the President of the U.S., George W. Bush, announced that all such cloning is unethical. He did not state the reason why it was deemed unethical. The pronouncement shows that the lack of a general moral maxim on which to base such decisions leads to…fuzzy morality.

69) Ira Levin, *"The Boys From Brazil,"* Random House, Inc., February 1976.

70) Michael C. Brannigan, *"Ethical Issues in Human Cloning,"* Seven Bridges Press, LLC, March 2000.

71) Leon R. Cass and James Q. Wilson, *"The Ethics of Human Cloning,"* AEI Press, July 1998.

72) Arthur Kaplan and Glenn McGee ed., *"The Human Cloning Debate,"* Berkeley Hills Books, May 2000.

73) James A. Byrne and John B. Gordon, *"Commentary on Human Cloning,"* Differentiation, 69, pp.154-57.

74) Stuart Hampshire, *"Public and Private Morality,"* Cambridge University Press, October 1978.

75) A. A. Thomas Mappes and Jane S. Zembaty, *"Social Ethics, Morality and Social Policy,"* McGraw-Hill Pub. Co., August 2001.

76) Luc Boltanski and Graham Burchell (translator), *"Distant Suffering: Morality, Media and Politics,"* Cambridge University Press, May 1999.

77) John David Skrentny, *"The Ironies of Affirmative Action: Politics, Culture, and Justice in America,"* University of Chicago Press, February 1995.

78) Sissela Bok, *"Lying: Moral Choice in Public and Private Life,"* Alfred A. Knopf, September 1999.

79) Aldert Vrij, *"Detecting Lies and Deceit: The Psychology of Lying and the Implications for Professional Practice,"* John Wiley and Sons, Inc., March 2000.

ABOUT THE AUTHOR

Dr. Nicolaos S. Tzannes holds a Ph.D in Electrical Engineering Science, Mathematics and Statistics from The Johns Hopkins University, Baltimore, Maryland. He also holds Bachelor's and Master's degrees from the University of Minnesota and Syracuse University, respectively. He is presently a professor of electrical engineering at the University of Central Florida, Orlando, Florida where he also chaired the Department from 1986-1994. He has taught at The Johns Hopkins University, Tufts University, the University of Oklahoma, the University of Virginia, Oregon State University and the University of Patras, Greece. Besides the books listed below, Dr. Tzannes has authored, co-authored or edited many other books and dozens of scientific papers in English and other languages.

Dr. Tzannes and his wife live part of the year in Orlando, Florida, and part of it in Kato Kastritsi, Greece. Yet another part of the year they spend visiting their three sons and their families, enjoying their six—so far—grandchildren. They devote the rest of the year to traveling around the globe.

OTHER BOOKS BY THE AUTHOR

Communication and Radar Systems, Prentice-Hall, 1985. Reprinted by iuniverse, Inc., 2000.

How Good Are You At Backgammon? (with B. Tzannes), Simon and Schuster, 1974. Revised and Re-issued by Writers Club Press, 2001.

Backgammon Games and Strategies (with B. Tzannes), Barnes and Co. 1977. Reprinted by toExcel Press, 2000.

As Aris P. D'Avenal (his pseudonym)

The Gene Conspiracy or *Sorry...the Genes Made Me Do It*, Writers Club Press, 2000.

10.03
19.95

T 535916

Printed in the United States
1281100001B/314

9 781591 297697